Monday Nights in JERUSALEM

JANET BURNINGHAM

Dedicated to Joshua and Benjamin

Monday Nights in JERUSALEM

Stories and Lessons for Family Home Evening
Based on the Old Testament

JANET BURNINGHAM

CFI
Springville, Utah

ISBN 978-1-59955-377-1

Published by CFI, an imprint of Cedar Fort, Inc., 2373 W. 700 S., Springville, UT, 84663
Distributed by Cedar Fort, Inc., www.cedarfort.com

Cover design by Megan Whittier
Edited and typeset by Heidi Doxey
Cover design © 2009 by Lyle Mortimer
Illustrations by Spencer Wood

Printed in the United States of America

10 9 8 7 6 5 4 3 2 1

Printed on acid-free paper

Contents

Acknowledgments

I'd like to thank everyone at Cedar Fort, Inc. for their patience in allowing me to complete this book. Without their encouragement and belief in me, it would still be sitting unfinished in my computer. They are wonderful people to work with, and I'm grateful for the opportunity to be a part of their team.

I offer a big thanks to my children for allowing me the time to read, study, and type on my computer in between feeding and taking care of them. They are my biggest cheerleaders!

And most especially, I offer my greatest thanks to my Heavenly Father for giving me the wisdom, strength, and inspiration to write this book under very difficult circumstances. He has blessed me beyond what I deserve.

Introduction

The purpose of this book is to help bring families to the scriptures. Through the scriptures we learn about the word of God and His plan for His children. The Old Testament teaches us about why we are here and what God expects from each of us; it also contains stories of those who have followed God's plan and have been blessed, and those who have ignored His counsel and have reaped sorrow.

Our children live in a fast-paced world where they want instant gratification. The scriptures teach us that God's blessings are almost never instantaneous. Instead, He tests our sincerity and our faith by allowing difficult things to happen to us to see if we will still love Him and believe in Him. This is an important principle for us and our children to learn in this day and age.

Taking the time to read the scriptures and have family home evening together can be difficult. We, as parents, are pulled in many different directions and, like our children, we often lack the motivation to read the scriptures. Making scripture study a priority in our lives is not always easy and does not always give immediate rewards, but it is a commandment. And like all commandments, we and our families will be blessed by keeping it.

I challenge you to commit to studying the scriptures with your family on a regular basis. As you do so, you will begin to notice a different spirit in your home. But don't forget that the adversary is against this practice and will place roadblocks in front of you. He does not want the spirit of the Lord in your home. However, press on, be diligent and faithful, and you and your family will reap the rewards. I have experienced this in my own home and promise that you will too!

How to Use This Book

Hi! My name is Simeon, and I am a scripture guide. You might remember me from *Monday Nights in Zarahemla* and *Monday Nights in Nauvoo* where I helped guide you through the Book of Mormon and the Doctrine and Covenants. I'm excited to be with you now as you journey through the Old Testament. The stories in the Old Testament are about faith, courage, and righteousness—all of which we need to develop in our lives if we want to return to our Heavenly Father one day. I hope you grow in understanding and enjoy your journey through the exciting stories of the Old Testament.

In each of the lessons you will find the following:

OBJECTIVE

Each lesson starts with a question that applies to the main message. Begin by asking the question to give the children a purpose in listening to the story.

STORY

Before beginning each lesson, make sure you read the summarizing story, which often contains background information about events and people that might not be covered in the verses. For younger children, you might want to read just the story and answer the questions, along with reading a few key verses. This will help them gain an understanding of the objective you are trying to teach without having to read all the verses.

GOSPEL ART PICTURE KIT (GAK):

When applicable, this references which picture from the Church's Gospel Art Picture Kit would correspond well with the lesson. You can hold or display a picture while studying the lesson. The back of each picture includes information that might be helpful to read aloud in addition to the lesson.

MAKE YOUR OWN GAK

A great summarizing activity is to have children draw a picture of the story on one side of a paper and have older children or a parent write a summary on the other side. Place these pages in a plastic page protector and put in a three-ring binder to read at home or at church. Children love looking at their own work and sharing it with others. Drawing pictures also helps them remember the lessons better.

WORD QUEST

Learning the language of the scriptures is important in being able to understand them. In each lesson you will find a list of words or phrases. Most children enjoy having a word or two assigned to them to look for while reading. When you get to each word, stop and talk about the meaning. Easy-to-understand definitions for the Word Quest words are given in the Treasures of Knowledge section.

VERSES

Only the verses that pertain to the story being studied are included in each lesson. Many verses and chapters that are repetitive or not relevant to the story are skipped over so as not to overwhelm the children. Parents are encouraged to read additional chapters and verses that they feel would benefit their family.

A series of simple comprehension and application questions are provided for each lesson. There are several ways in which the verses and questions can be studied, and parents should read as little or as much as they think their family will enjoy. It is recommended that you first read the questions before reading the verses; this helps increase attention and comprehension. In my family, we read the story first and then ask the questions. We then read through the verses and try to answer the questions we didn't know from the story. My children seem more motivated to read when we follow this pattern.

TREASURES OF KNOWLEDGE

Included in each lesson are comments or explanations which may further enhance your understanding of the scriptural passages you have read. Parents are encouraged to read these explanations and talk about them with their children. Important discussions will often take place when teaching these gospel truths to your children. The definitions for the words listed in the Word Quest are also found here.

What Are the Bible, the JST, and the Pearl of Great Price?

WHAT IS THE BIBLE?

The Bible is a collection of books that were written by many different authors over a period of more than a thousand years. It has been translated and retranslated into several different languages over the years. It is God's word to His children, and it begins with the Creation of the world. Most of the Bible is written about the Israelites, God's chosen people, who came from a man named Israel, the grandson of Abraham, a descendant of Noah. Israel is introduced in the book of Genesis and the remainder of the Bible is written about his descendants. The books are arranged by type: the five books of Moses and the law; the history of the Israelites; books of wisdom; and books of the prophets.

WHAT IS THE JST (JOSEPH SMITH TRANSLATION)?

Long ago, there were no printed books; each book had to be handwritten and copied from another source. This made it very easy for mistakes to be made and for anyone to change the text if they didn't like what it said. This is what happened with the Bible as it was copied over and over again throughout the years. Because of these errors, the Lord commanded Joseph Smith to read through the Bible and retranslate it. With the spirit of the Lord guiding him, Joseph was able to add words that were left out, change words and phrases that were wrong, and correctly interpret verses and passages. Because of this translation, many important truths were restored to the earth again.

WHAT IS THE PEARL OF GREAT PRICE?

The Pearl of Great Price was originally a publication

made by Franklin D. Richards in the early days of the church. When he was translating the Bible, Joseph Smith made many changes to the book of Genesis. Brother Richards wanted the early Saints to read about the changes Joseph had made, so he published a booklet to hand out to members of the Church in England, where he was serving at the time. The book of Moses and the book of Abraham are two books in the Pearl of Great Price that we will study in this guide. The book of Moses is a translation of the first six chapters of the book of Genesis, originally written by Moses, and the book of Abraham is a translation of some Egyptian papers that Joseph Smith received. They contain important truths about our premortal life and the life of Abraham.

Lessons

LESSON ONE

Our Premortal Life

STORY

Long ago, there were prophets who were shown visions of Heavenly Father's spirit children before they came to earth. Abraham and Moses were two of these prophets, and in their visions, Abraham and Moses were shown very special spirits called the "noble and great ones," who were chosen to be spiritual rulers and leaders while living on the earth. Many of these spirits were able to help Heavenly Father and Jesus create the earth. Abraham was told that he was one of these noble and great spirits.

From both of these visions, we learn that we once lived with our Heavenly parents as spirit children. Heavenly Father knew that it was time for us to come to earth, to receive mortal bodies, and to be tested to see if we would "do all things whatsoever the Lord (our) God shall command" (Abraham 3:25) us to do. If we chose to follow Heavenly Father with an honest heart while we were on earth, then we would be able to return to live with Him again after we died.

WORD QUEST
- intelligence
- first estate
- second estate
- added upon
- redeem
- Beloved

Since Heavenly Father knew we would make mistakes, He presented a plan that would allow us to repent (change) and keep trying. His plan required a Savior to show us the way to live and to pay for our sins. Two of our spirit brothers wanted to "save" us: Jesus Christ, and Lucifer. However, Lucifer wanted to save us by forcing us to choose the right, to "destroy the agency of man." Lucifer also wanted to receive all the glory for his plan instead of giving the honor and glory to Heavenly Father.

Jesus said, "Here am I, send me." He wanted to follow Heavenly Father's plan—to let us choose for ourselves whom we would serve. Jesus offered to sacrifice His life on earth and to give the glory to God.

When Heavenly Father chose to send Jesus Christ to earth, Lucifer and his followers became very angry. Because of their rebellion from God, Lucifer and those who followed him were cast out of Heavenly Father's presence and were not allowed to come to earth to gain bodies.

Lucifer is also called the devil or "the father of all lies." He and his followers have been trying since the beginning to "deceive and to blind men, and to lead them" away from following God's commands. Lucifer wants all of Heavenly Father's spirit children to fail and be miserable like he is. His greatest desire is to keep us from returning to our Heavenly Father, which is why it is so important to learn about Heavenly Father and what we need to do to return to Him one day.

VERSES	SUGGESTED QUESTIONS	TREASURES OF KNOWLEDGE
Abraham 3:22–28 **Moses: 4:1–4**	• What were the special spirits called that Abraham saw? (Abraham 3:22) • What was one of the reasons we were sent to earth? (Abraham 3:25) • How are you doing with this test on earth? What changes might you need to make to do better? • Did Jesus want the glory for following Heavenly Father's plan? (Moses 4:2) • What were the differences between Satan's plan and God's plan? (Moses 4:1–2) • Why do you think Satan's plan would have been bad for us? • Why is freedom so important? • How did Satan react to God choosing Jesus? (Abraham 3:28) • Were there others who followed Satan, and if so, what happened to them? (Abraham 3:28) • What does Satan try to do to us? (Moses 4:4) • How can your knowledge of Heavenly Father's plan help you fight against Satan? Name some specific things you can do to make sure he doesn't lead you away from God.	**intelligence:** what we were before we were spirits. Our intelligence has no beginning and no end. **first estate:** our first home in the spirit world **second estate:** our home here on earth **added upon:** allowed to continue their progression **redeem:** to save from the consequences of sin **Beloved:** one who is deeply loved **"one among them that was like unto God":** a reference to Jesus Christ.

LESSON TWO

The Work and Glory of God

STORY

Moses was a prophet from the Old Testament who spoke to God face to face. Jesus Christ is the God of the Old Testament; he is Jehovah. However, when he speaks to His prophets, He speaks as if he were the Father. Moses was allowed to see Jesus and talk to Him because he was transfigured—meaning changes were temporarily made to his body which allowed him to be in the presence of God. From talking to God, Moses learned that God is endless, "without beginning of days or end of years" and that Moses was God's son, one of His great creations.

Moses was shown a grand vision of the world and of all the children God created. Before Moses saw all of God's creations, he had been a prince in the mighty land of Egypt. He had seen all the power and glory of men, but after receiving this vision, Moses realized how powerless men really are and how great the glory of God is.

After Moses's vision, he was very tired, and it took many hours before he got his strength back. After the spirit of God left him, Satan appeared to Moses, trying to tempt him. After seeing the wondrous glory of God, the power of Satan paled in comparison, yet Satan still wanted Moses to worship him. But Moses had been told

WORD QUEST
- son of man
- similitude
- Only Begotten
- immortality
- eternal life

by God that he was a son of God, like His son Jesus Christ, and Moses could tell the difference between God's glory and Satan's. Even though Satan was a being from the spirit world with powers that might impress someone else, Moses knew the difference between his and God's glory.

When Moses told Satan to leave him alone, Satan became very angry and yelled and cried out in a loud voice demanding that Moses worship him. Satan's anger scared Moses; nevertheless, he knew that God's power was greater, so he called upon God for help, and God gave him the strength to command Satan to leave by saying, "In the name of the Only Begotten, *depart* hence, *Satan*." This made Satan so angry that his trembling caused the earth to shake, but because he had been commanded to leave in Jesus's name Satan had to obey, and he left Moses alone.

After Satan left, Moses prayed again to God, asking Him to tell Moses more about His creations. God explained to Moses that He has created so many worlds and heavens that Moses would not be able to count them, yet God knows each and every one of His creations. Of all these works, God's greatest work is His spirit children. And His greatest glory is seeing His children receive the gift of immortality—the reuniting of spirits and bodies after death—and the gift of eternal life, which is to have life with and be like God for all eternity.

Moses's vision teaches us that we are known and loved by our Heavenly Father, and that if we keep His commandments and try our best, we can live with Him again for all eternity!

VERSES	SUGGESTED QUESTIONS	TREASURES OF KNOWLEDGE
Moses 1:1–4, 8–13, 16, 19–24, 36–40	• How was Moses able to be in God's presence? (v. 2) • Name three things God either told or showed to Moses when he spoke to Him face to face? (vv. 3, 4, 8) • How long was it until Moses got his strength back after the presence of God withdrew? (v. 10) • Who appeared to Moses after his vision, and what did that person say? (v. 12) • Did Satan have glory like God? (v. 13) • What did Moses tell Satan to do? (v. 16) • What did Satan do when Moses told him to leave? (v. 19) • Was Moses afraid of Satan? (v. 20) • Where did Moses receive the strength to tell Satan to depart? (v. 20) • Why do you think Satan had to leave when he was commanded to in Jesus's name? • How can knowing this help you when you're afraid? • What event is God prophesying about in verse 25? (the parting of the Red Sea) • Has God created more than one heaven and earth? Is it possible for man to count them? (vv. 37–38)	**man is nothing:** This does not mean that we are worth nothing; instead, it refers to our dependence on God to deliver us from our sins and allow us to live with him again. No one can be saved without God's power. We are not able to save ourselves on our own. **son of man:** God told Moses he was a "son of God" but Satan referred to him as a "son of man." Satan was trying to knock Moses down, to make him feel that he was nothing important. **similitude:** similar; Moses's role in freeing the Israelites from captivity was similar to Jesus's role in freeing us from Satan when we sin. **Only Begotten:** Jesus Christ; even though Jesus is the one speaking to Moses, he is speaking for the Father, and so he speaks as if he were the Father. **"in the name of Jesus Christ":** Only through the power of Jesus Christ was Moses able to command Satan to depart. Only through the power of Jesus Christ can we fight against Satan in our own lives.

VERSES	SUGGESTED QUESTIONS	TREASURES OF KNOWLEDGE
Moses 1:1–4, 8–13, 16, 19–24, 36–40	• Next time you look at a picture of space, remember these verses and what you learned about God's endless creations. • What is God's work and glory? (v. 39) • What is the difference between immortality and eternal life? (see Treasures of Knowledge)	**"my work and my glory":** Heavenly Father's purpose for sending us to earth. **immortality:** the reuniting of body and spirit after death to never be separated again **eternal life:** living with and being like Heavenly Father forever

LESSON THREE

The Creation

GOSPEL ART PICTURE KIT

100

STORY:

In the previous lesson, we discussed how Moses spokc to God and learned about the Creation of our earth. God commanded Moses to write those teachings down, and they are recorded in the book of Moses, which is found in the Pearl of Great Price. The book of Moses is a translation made by the Prophet Joseph Smith of the book of Genesis in the Old Testament.

Jesus Christ, under the direction of Heavenly Father, created this earth with the help of Michael, who later became the first man on earth—Adam. Jesus and Michael did not create the earth out of nothing; they organized it into the form it is now. All the elements used to create the earth were already in existence. The organization of the earth was divided up into six different periods of time, or "days," but in this case, the word "day" does not mean the same amount of time as our day; it is much longer.

WORD QUEST

- day
- firmament
- subdue
- dominion
- sanctified

During the first creative period, Heavenly Father instructed Jesus and Michael to divide the light from the darkness. "And I God, called the light day; and the darkness I called night" (Moses 2:5). During the second period, Jesus and Michael organized and separated the waters, and on the third day they organized the dry land, with all the plant life such as trees, flowers, and bushes. During the fourth period, Jesus and Michael created the sun, the moon, and the stars. The sun was made to rule over the day, and the moon was made to rule over the night.

Jesus and Michael also created the fishes, whales, and birds during the fifth period; and during the sixth period they created all other animals that live upon the earth. They told the animals "to be fruitful and multiply the earth" which means to have babies and fill the earth with their own kind.

Michael was then given a body, a body that looked like our Heavenly Father. Adam was chosen to come to earth and live in a beautiful place called the "Garden of Eden." After he came to earth, a veil of forgetfulness was placed over his mind, and he no longer remembered he was Michael or that he had helped organize the earth.

After all these periods of creation, Jesus and Heavenly Father saw that their works were good, and they rested during the seventh period.

VERSES	SUGGESTED QUESTIONS	TREASURES OF KNOWLEDGE
Moses 2:1–31; Moses 3:1–3	• Who did the Lord tell about the Creation of the earth? (Moses 2:1) • Who created this earth? (see story) • What did God (and Jesus and Michael) do on the first "day"? (Moses 2:4) • What did God call the light and the dark? (Moses 2:5) • What did God do on the second day? (Moses 2:6–7) • What did God call the firmament? (Moses 2:8 and footnote 8a) • What did God call the "dry land"? (Moses 2:10 and footnote 10a)	**"this heaven and this earth":** God has created numberless worlds. In this chapter, He is explaining the creation of this earth only. **day:** a period of time; we do not know how long each day was. **firmament:** everything above the earth—the sky, the stars, the atmosphere **subdue:** to prepare the land for growing things **dominion:** to have authority over something and to take care of it **sanctified:** to make holy or sacred

VERSES	SUGGESTED QUESTIONS	TREASURES OF KNOWLEDGE
	• What did God create on the third day? (Moses 2:11,12) • What did God create on the fourth day? (Moses 2:16) • What did God create on the fifth day? (Moses 2:21) • What did God tell the creatures to do? (Moses 2:22) • Who did God create on the sixth day? (Moses 2:27) • What did God command Adam to do? (Moses 2:28) • What did God do on the seventh day? (Moses 3:2, 3)	

OPTIONAL ACTIVITY

Have each family member divide a sheet of paper into six parts and write or draw pictures of what God created on each day. Talk about each day, and have everyone tell which of God's creations they are grateful for and why.

LESSON FOUR

Adam and Eve

GOSPEL ART PICTURE KIT

101

STORY

In the previous lesson, we learned that Jesus Christ and Michael created the earth under the direction of Heavenly Father. Michael was chosen to come to earth as the first human and was given the name of Adam. Heavenly Father and Jesus also created a partner for Adam, a woman named Eve.

Adam and Eve were given a home in the Garden of Eden, a beautiful paradise filled with a variety of plants and animals. God commanded Adam and Eve to take care of the plants and animals and to enjoy living there. They were told that they could eat all the fruits and vegetables except for one—the fruit from a tree called "the tree of knowledge of good and evil." God told Adam and Eve that if they ate the fruit from that tree, they would die (meaning they would become mortal and would have to leave the garden of Eden); however, God also told them they could choose to eat it if they wanted. The reason God gave them the choice was that He knew the consequences of becoming mortal, and He wanted Adam

WORD QUEST
- help meet
- aprons
- beguiled
- transgression

and Eve to choose for themselves if this was what they really wanted. Heavenly Father wanted to give us the opportunity to be like Him, but it had to be our choice. If God had told them they could eat the fruit, then they could blame him for all the hardships and pains of mortality. It had to be their choice, not His.

While Adam and Eve were living in the garden, Satan, through a serpent, spoke to Eve. God allowed Satan to enter the garden to tempt Adam and Eve so they could choose for themselves if they wanted to stay or if they wanted to become mortal. However, Satan did not know this, and he saw an opportunity to destroy the plan of God. He knew that if Adam and Eve ate the fruit, they would be cast out of the Garden of Eden and become mortal.

In the Garden, their bodies were different from the way ours are now. They couldn't get sick and they couldn't die. And because they were innocent and didn't know the difference between right and wrong, they couldn't sin. But Satan knew that once they were mortal, they could sin, and he wanted to tempt them as mortals to break God's commandments, which would keep them from returning to God. Satan's greatest pleasure is keeping any of Heavenly Father's children away from Him—both in this life, and in the eternities.

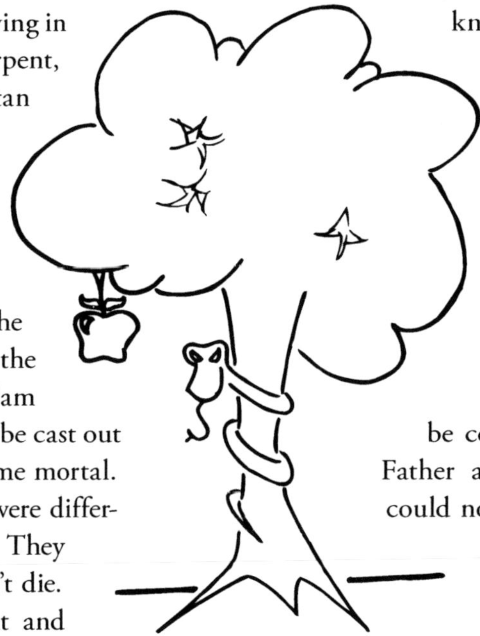

Satan, through the serpent, succeeded in getting Eve to eat the fruit. Eve desired to be like our Heavenly Father, and Satan told her that if she ate the fruit, she would be "as the gods, knowing good and evil" (Moses 4:11). Eve chose to eat the fruit because she knew it was the only way to become like Heavenly Father. She knew that she would become mortal and be subject to death and disease, but she also knew the eternal reward for passing through mortality. After eating the fruit, Eve went to Adam and got him to eat the fruit also.

Afterwards, Adam and Eve realized what they had done and tried to hide from God, knowing He would be coming to visit them. When Heavenly Father and Jesus came to the garden, they could not find Adam and Eve and they knew that Adam and Eve were hiding. God asked Adam and Eve if they had eaten of the forbidden fruit, and they admitted that they had. Because of this transgression, they had to leave the garden and their bodies became mortal, which meant they were now able to bear children and could keep Heavenly Father's commandment to "multiply and replenish the earth."

VERSES	SUGGESTED QUESTIONS	TREASURES OF KNOWLEDGE
Moses 3:8, 16–18, 21–22	• Adam was commanded to not eat the fruit of which tree? (v. 17) • What did God say would happen if Adam chose to eat the fruit? (v. 17) • Why did God want a companion for Adam? (v. 18)	**Was Eve created from Adam's rib?** "Modern prophets have taught that the creation of woman from the rib of the man is to be taken figuratively; a rib being a metaphor for a person corresponding to Adam" (Seely, 1994). **help meet:** "The original Hebrew for *meet* means that Eve was adequate for, or equal to, Adam. She wasn't his servant or his subordinate. And the Hebrew for *help* in "help meet" is *ezer,* a term meaning that Eve drew on heavenly powers when she supplied their marriage with the spiritual instincts uniquely available to women as a gender gift" (Hafen 2007).
Moses 4:6–19, 26	• What was Adam's wife's name? (v. 26) • What did Satan ask Eve? (vv. 7, 10) • Why did Eve decide to eat the fruit? (v. 12) • Did Adam also choose to eat the fruit? (v. 12)	**aprons:** clothes **beguiled:** deceived

VERSES	SUGGESTED QUESTIONS	TREASURES OF KNOWLEDGE
Moses 4:6–19, 26	• What happened after they ate the fruit? (v. 13) • What did Adam and Eve do when they heard the Lord's voice? (v. 14) Why do you think they did this? • How do you think God knew that Adam had eaten the fruit? • Who did Adam blame for eating the fruit? (v. 18) • Who did Eve blame? (v. 19)	
Moses 4:27–31	• Did Adam and Eve have to leave the garden? (v. 29)	**transgression:** a broken commandment

LESSON FIVE

Cain and Abel

GOSPEL ART PICTURE KIT

119

STORY:

After leaving the Garden of Eden, Adam and Eve continued to worship the Lord and received instructions from an angel about the plan of salvation and the law of sacrifice. Adam and Eve had many children before they received these instructions and when they tried to teach the gospel to their children, some of their children did not believe them. Satan had influenced the hearts of their children and told them not to believe in God. This made Adam and Eve very sad because they remembered what it was like to live with Heavenly Father. Adam and Eve wanted each of their children to experience that joy for themselves one day.

Adam and Eve later gave birth to a son named Cain and then a son named Abel. Adam and Eve hoped that if they taught their sons the gospel early on, they would follow its principles and worship God. In fact, Cain was the first of Adam's children to receive the priesthood from his father, who had received it from the Lord. As a mortal, Cain had a personal relationship with the Lord

WORD QUEST
- sweat of his brow
- firstlings
- keeper of sheep
- tiller of the ground
- offering

and spoke to Him. However, Satan got a hold of Cain's heart, and Cain began to love Satan more than God. Satan somehow convinced Cain that being a keeper of the flocks, which is what Abel did, was more important than being in charge of the crops and that God must love Abel more. Cain then became jealous of Abel, and Satan took advantage of this jealousy by telling Cain to offer a sacrifice of the fruits of the field to God, knowing that it would not be acceptable. Cain followed Satan's request and offered a sacrifice of the land. Of course, the Lord did not accept Cain's offering, but he did accept Abel's offering of a lamb.

Cain became so jealous and angry with Abel that Satan convinced him to kill Abel so that Cain could be the keeper of the land. Cain killed Abel in secret. When God came to speak to Cain, He asked him where Abel was. Cain responded that he did not know; he said "I know not. Am I my brother's *keeper*?" (Moses 5:34).

But God knew Cain had killed Abel. He told Cain that he would be cursed and that Cain could never come back into His presence because he chose to serve Satan. Cain was very upset with his punishment and told God, "Satan *tempted* me because of my brother's flocks. And I was wroth also; for his offering thou didst accept and not mine; my *punishment* is greater than I can bear" (Moses 5:38). Nevertheless, because of Cain's rebellion against God he was "shut out from the presence of the Lord" forever (Moses 5:41). Afterwards, Cain took his wife and family and left to live in another part of the land, away from many of Adam and Eve's children.

VERSES	SUGGESTED QUESTIONS	TREASURES OF KNOWLEDGE
Moses 5:1–2, 16–21	• What were the names of Adam's and Eve's sons? (vv. 16–17) • What were Cain's and Abel's different responsibilities? (v. 17) • Who did Cain love more than God? (v. 18) • What did Satan tell Cain to offer to God? (v. 18) • What was Abel's offering to God? (v. 20) • Whose offering did God accept? (v. 20) • Why do you think God did not accept Cain's offering? (see "Treasures of Knowledge") • How did Cain feel about God not accepting his offering? (v. 21) • Who did Cain decide to stop listening to? (v. 26) • Why were Adam and Eve sad? (v. 27) • Why do you think parents are sad when their children choose to not follow God?	**sweat of his brow:** In the Garden of Eden, fruits and vegetables grew naturally, but in the mortal world, Adam had to work hard to dig the soil, plant the seeds, and harvest the crops. **firstlings:** first-born male animal **keeper of sheep:** someone who takes care of the animals. **tiller of the ground:** someone who takes care of the crops.

VERSES	SUGGESTED QUESTIONS	TREASURES OF KNOWLEDGE
Moses 5:32–25, 38–41	• What did Cain do to Abel? (v. 32) • What did Cain think he would get after Abel was gone? (v. 33) • What was Cain's response when God asked him where Abel was? (v. 34) • What was Cain's "excuse" for killing Abel? (v. 38) • What happened to Cain and where did he go? (v. 41)	**offering:** to present something to God as an act of worship **Why did people make animal sacrifices to God?** Adam and Eve were commanded to sacrifice, by the shedding of blood, the first-born male animal as a symbolic reminder of the future sacrifice of Jesus Christ, who is Heavenly Father's first-born son. **Why was Cain's sacrifice of crops not acceptable?** The sacrifice of fruits and vegetables is not similar to the sacrifice of Jesus Christ, and it was not what God had commanded Cain to sacrifice.

LESSON SIX

Enoch and the City of Zion

GOSPEL ART PICTURE KIT

120

STORY:

Enoch was a righteous man who lived hundreds of years after Adam. Enoch was Adam's great-great-great-great-great-grandson. When Enoch was still young, God called him to be a prophet and to tell the wicked people to repent and to serve the Lord, who created them. Enoch did not feel that he was ready to be a prophet because he was so young, and he also had a speech problem that people made fun of. But God told Enoch that He would give Enoch the ability to speak and to preach the gospel.

Enoch spent many years preaching the gospel throughout the land. There were many who believed him and were baptized. All the believers gathered together to live in a city called Zion. Zion became a righteous city where the pure in heart lived and there was no poor among them. Even though many people believed in God and followed His commandments, there were many more people who were wicked and fought against the people of God.

After many years, God showed Enoch a vision

Do you think God is sad when we make bad decisions?

WORD QUEST

- hearts waxed hard
- ears are dull of hearing
- eyes cannot see afar off
- one heart, one mind
- cursed
- bowels yearned
- Son of Man
- Righteous Lamb
- translated

where he saw the city of Zion and all the inhabitants taken up into heaven because they were so righteous. Enoch was also shown the rest of the people who were left on the earth and who were wicked. Enoch saw that God cried because of the sins of His children, and Enoch did not understand why God would cry. God explained, "[these people are] the workmanship of mine own *hands*, and I gave unto them [a] commandment, that they should *love* one another, and that they should choose me, their Father; but behold, they are without affection, and they *hate* their own blood." (Moses 7:32–33)

The wickedness of the people made Enoch cry too when he saw the pain that they would one day be in if they did not repent. But God comforted Enoch by showing him the future sacrifice of Jesus Christ. God explained to Enoch that all those who repented would be forgiven of their sins and allowed to live with God again. This gave Enoch great comfort in knowing how much God loves His children. After 365 years, the city of Enoch was translated, and all its inhabitants were taken up to heaven to live with God.

VERSES	SUGGESTED QUESTIONS	TREASURES OF KNOWLEDGE
Moses 6:26–27, 31–33	• What did God call Enoch to do? (v. 27) • Why was God angry with the people? (v. 27) • Are there times when you don't listen to God? Do you ever think about how your actions affect how God feels? • Name two reasons why Enoch did not feel worthy to be a prophet. (v. 31) • How does it make you feel to know that God will give you the strength to keep His commandments? • Is choosing to serve God a choice? What other choice do we have? Have you chosen to serve God or are you still deciding?	**"hearts waxed hard":** to ignore the promptings of the Spirit **"ears are dull of hearing":** to not listen to the word of God or His prophets **"eyes cannot see afar off":** to live in the moment and not "see" the future consequences of your sins. **"one heart, one mind":** unity—when people care about others as much as, if not more than, themselves. **"the people have I cursed":** This means that the people will no longer receive God's help and his mercy; they have chosen to be alone and will have to suffer the consequences of their sins.

VERSES	SUGGESTED QUESTIONS	TREASURES OF KNOWLEDGE
Moses 7:18–21, 28–29, 32–33, 41, 44, 47, 67–69	• What was the name of the city where Enoch and his people lived? (v. 19) • What were the people of Zion like? (v. 18) • Would you like to live in a place like Zion? If so, what kind of changes do you need to make so you could live there? • Why did God cry and feel sad about the wicked people on earth? (v. 32–33) • How does it make you feel to know God cries and feels sad? • What was Enoch's response to the wickedness of men? (vv. 41, 44) • When Enoch was sad, what did the Lord show him to comfort him? (v. 47) • How many years was the city of Enoch on the earth? (v. 68) • What happened to the city of Zion? (v. 69)	**bowels yearned:** very strong, sad emotions **Son of Man:** God the Father is the "Man of Holiness" and so Jesus Christ, His son, is the "Son of Man of Holiness," or the "Son of Man." (McConkie, 742) **The Righteous Lamb:** Jesus Christ—He was sacrificed, like a lamb, by the shedding of blood. **What does it mean to be translated?** According to the prophet Joseph Smith, "many may have supposed that the doctrine of translation was a doctrine whereby men were taken immediately into the presence of God and into an eternal fullness. But this is a mistaken idea. Their place of habitation is that of the terrestrial order and a place prepared for such . . . he held in reserve to be ministering angels . . . and who as yet have not entered into so great a fullness as those who are resurrected from the dead." (Jackson, 20)

LESSON SEVEN

Noah

GOSPEL ART PICTURE KIT

102, 103

STORY:

In this story we are introduced to a man named Noah, the great-grandson of Enoch. Noah was called by the Lord to preach repentance to the wicked people left on earth after the city of Zion was translated. But like many prophets before and after him, Noah was rejected by the people. This made God very sad, and He said to Noah, "The end of all flesh is come before me, for the earth is filled with violence, and behold I will *destroy* all flesh from off the earth" (Moses 8:30). God had decided to send a great flood of water to destroy all living things.

This might sound like a mean thing for a loving God to do, but it was actually an act of mercy, or kindness. There were many spirits who were waiting to come to earth to gain a body, but they knew that they would be sent into a wicked home since there were no righteous people on the earth besides Noah's family. We learned in a previous lesson that God's purpose in sending us here is to give us a chance to have eternal life, but that could not happen if the people rejected the gospel. Because of

WORD QUEST
- pitch
- token
- covenant
- perpetual

this, the Lord needed to bring a new, righteous generation to earth to send his spirit children to. Another reason the flood was a merciful act was that it kept the wicked from committing further sins and from passing those sinful habits on to their children and grandchildren. If they had passed on their sinful traditions, they would have been held accountable for their children's sins one day. (Church Educational System, 56)

To prepare for the flood, God commanded Noah to build an ark and to collect animals and food of every kind. He saved a male and female of each animal so that after the flood they could have babies and continue to fill the earth with their own kind. Noah was also told to take his family with him on the ark. After they were all safely on the ark, the rains and floods began to cover the earth. It rained for forty days and forty nights straight, but it took about a year before Noah was able to leave the ark again.

After the flood, God made a covenant with Noah that He would never flood the earth again. He told Noah that the rainbow would serve as a reminder to Noah and all future generations of this covenant.

VERSES	SUGGESTED QUESTIONS	TREASURES OF KNOWLEDGE
Moses 8:19–20, 27–30	• What was Noah commanded to do first? (v. 19) • Did the people listen to Noah and repent? (v. 20) • What kind of man was Noah? (v. 27) • Describe what the people on earth were like during this time. (v. 28) • What did God tell Noah He was going to do because the people were so wicked? (v. 30)	

VERSES	SUGGESTED QUESTIONS	TREASURES OF KNOWLEDGE
Genesis 6:14, 19–21	• What did God command Noah to build? (v. 14) • What was Noah told to put in the ark with him? (v. 19) • Name three types of animals Noah was told to take on the ark. (v. 20)	**"perfect in his generation":** The footnote for this verse states that perfect means "complete, whole, having integrity" (See Genesis 6:9 footnote c). **pitch:** a dark substance used for sealing the boat to protect it from getting water inside
Genesis 7:4, 7, 17–18, 23–24	• Who survived the flood? (v. 23) • How long did the water "prevail" on the earth? (v. 24)	**The number forty in the Bible:** You will notice in your study of the Bible that the number forty appears frequently. Some scholars believe that the number forty signifies simply a large number, so forty days would mean a long period of time and not literally forty days.
Genesis 8:14–17	• When did the earth become dry again? (v. 14)	
Genesis 9:8–9, 12–17	• What was the symbol of the covenant God made between Noah and all future generations? (vv. 12–14) • Will God ever send another flood to destroy the people on the earth again? (v. 15)	**token:** an outward sign of a promise made **covenant:** a two-way promise between God and man **perpetual:** continuing

LESSON EIGHT

Abraham

GOSPEL ART PICTURE KIT

104

STORY

Hundreds of years after the flood lived a descendent of Noah named Abram. Abram lived in the city of Ur, where many of the people did not worship the living God and instead worshipped false gods called idols. An idol is anything that is worshipped other than the one and only true God. The people of Ur sacrificed people to their gods; they thought that doing this would please their gods. Abram, however, was a righteous man who would not worship the false gods, so the wicked priests decided to sacrifice Abram to their gods. But Heavenly Father protected Abram and delivered him from the wicked priests. God commanded Abram and his family to leave the land of Ur because there would be a great famine in the land where no food would grow and the animals would die.

Abram took his family and his wife Sarai to Egypt where there was no famine. On their way to Egypt, they went through a land called Canaan. God promised Abram that his family and his future family would one day possess that land. God also promised Abram

WORD QUEST

- laughed
- seed
- bare
- circumcised

that he would be the father of many children and that his posterity, which is his grandchildren, great-grandchildren, and so on, would fill the nations of the earth. This was a marvelous blessing and one that Abram and his wife needed to have great faith in since Sarai was unable to have children. God also changed Abram's name to Abraham and Sarai's name to Sarah. Abraham and Sarah waited many years for God to bless Sarah with a child. Finally when Abraham was one hundred years old, a son named Isaac was born! Isaac would carry on the gospel covenant that Abraham had made with God and he would later pass it on to his son Jacob, who would pass it on to his son Joseph and his other eleven sons.

VERSES	SUGGESTED QUESTIONS	TREASURES OF KNOWLEDGE
Abraham 1:1, 5–8,12, 15–19, 29–30	• What did the people of Ur worship? (vv. 5, 7) • What did the priests want to do to Abram? (v. 12) • Why did God save Abram? (v. 15) • Why did Abram and his family leave Ur? (vv. 29–30)	
Genesis 12:1–5, 7	• Who went with Abram and where did they go? (v. 5) • Who appeared to Abram and what did He promise Abram? (v. 7)	**"in thee shall all families of the earth be blessed"** Abraham and his future children would preach the gospel of Jesus Christ to all the nations of the earth.
Genesis 17:1–5	• What did God promise Abram? (v. 4) • What do you think it means to be "a father of many nations"? • What did God change Abram's name to? (v. 5)	

VERSES	SUGGESTED QUESTIONS	TREASURES OF KNOWLEDGE
Genesis 17:15–17, 19	• What did God change Sarai's name to? (v. 15) • What did God promise to bless Sarah with? (v. 16) • How might you have felt if you were Sarah? Would you believe God's promise? • What was Abraham's response to God's promise? (v. 17)	**laughed:** rejoiced (see Genesis 17:17 footnote a) **seed:** descendents (grandchildren, great-grandchildren, and so forth)
Genesis 21:1–5	• Did the Lord keep his promise to Abraham and Sarah? (vv. 1–2) • How old was Abraham when Isaac was born? (v. 5) • Why was the birth of Isaac a miracle? • What does this story teach you about what God can do for you?	**bare:** gave birth to **circumcised:** a physical act performed on males that symbolizes a spiritual covenant

LESSON NINE

Abraham and Isaac

GOSPEL ART PICTURE KIT

105

STORY

In the previous story, we learned about Abraham and Sarah and their long wait for a son who finally blessed their lives when Abraham was one hundred years old. This special child's name was Isaac, and he was the covenant child, the one who would carry on the priesthood and whose posterity would help fill the nations of the earth. When Isaac was older, the Lord came to Abraham and commanded him to offer Isaac as a sacrifice. This meant that Isaac would be placed on an altar and killed as a sacrifice to God. The sacrifice of animals was something that God had commanded to be been done since the days of Adam as a symbolic act of the future sacrifice of Jesus Christ. But the sacrifice of humans was something God had said was wrong. In fact, when Abraham was a boy, he had lived in a wicked city that sacrificed people to their false gods. Abraham himself had almost been sacrificed but was saved by God and escaped the city.

God was now testing Abraham's faith by asking him to sacrifice his beloved son Isaac. This was a tremendous

WORD QUEST
- tempt
- clave

test for Abraham since he loved his son Isaac so much. But Abraham loved God more and knew that God wouldn't command him to do something unless there was a good reason for it.

Abraham obeyed God and took Isaac and two of his servants and journeyed for three days to Mount Moriah where the sacrifice would be made. When they reached the mountain, the servants stayed behind with the donkey, and Abraham and Isaac climbed the mountain. On the way to the mountain, Isaac carried the wood and asked his father where the animal was that they needed to sacrifice. Abraham told him that the Lord would provide.

Once they reached their destination, Abraham built an altar and placed Isaac on top of the wood. This was a test for Isaac too because Abraham was over one hundred years old at the time and Isaac was most likely an adult. Isaac would have had to willingly agree to be sacrificed by his father.

Just as Abraham was getting ready to kill his son, an angel appeared and told him to stop. The angel told Abraham that God had been testing his faith, to know if he loved God and would do anything he was commanded to do. Now God knew that Abraham was willing. A ram then appeared in the bushes; the ram was being given to Abraham as a replacement for Isaac's sacrifice.

Because of Abraham's great faith, the Lord again promised Abraham that his posterity would be as numerous as the stars in the sky and that they would bless every nation of the earth. This was a difficult test that Abraham passed, and he was blessed forever because of it.

The sacrifice that Abraham was asked to make was symbolic of Heavenly Father's willingness to let His Beloved Son, Jesus Christ, come to earth and be sacrificed upon a cross. Abraham could now understand the depth of God's love for all of His children in being willing to let His Son die for us.

VERSES	SUGGESTED QUESTIONS	TREASURES OF KNOWLEDGE
Genesis 22:1–19	• What did God ask Abraham to do? (v. 2) • What did Isaac ask Abraham? (v. 7) • What was Abraham's response to Isaac? (v. 8) • How do you think Abraham must have been feeling at this time? • What did Abraham do after he built the altar? (vv. 9–10) • How do you think Isaac was feeling at this time? • What did the angel say to Abraham? (v. 12) • What did God provide for Abraham to sacrifice instead of Isaac? (v. 13) • What was God's blessing to Abraham? (vv. 17–18) • What does the sacrifice of Isaac represent? (see story) • What would be the hardest thing for you to ever give up? Would you do it if God asked?	**tempt:** test or prove (see Genesis 22:1 footnote) **clave:** cut **"possess the gate of his enemies":** "among other things, this means that the righteous descendants of Abraham will triumph over all obstacles that stand in the way of exaltation" (Ridges, vol. 1, 297). **What blessings might Abraham have received for passing such a test?** The prophet Joseph Smith stated that "Abraham obtained power, even power of an endless life . . . by the offering of his son Isaac. If a man would attain, he must sacrifice all to attain to the keys of the kingdom of an endless life" (Jackson, 24).

LESSON TEN

Jacob and Esau

STORY:

When Isaac grew up, he married a woman named Rebekah. They had a difficult time having children, but they prayed to the Lord, and He blessed them with twin boys: Esau and Jacob. Esau was born first, so he was the birthright child. The person with the birthright would inherit a double portion of his father's land and would be in charge when his father died.

When Esau and Jacob grew up, they took on different responsibilities; Esau was a hunter, and Jacob stayed at home and took care of the land and animals. One day, Esau had come back from a long journey of hunting and wanted Jacob to give him some food. Jacob knew that Esau didn't care about the birthright or the land, so Jacob offered to give Esau some food if he would give Jacob the birthright. Since Esau thought so little of the blessing, he gave it to Jacob in exchange for the food.

Esau later married a woman outside of the covenant, which meant she did not believe in God or keep His commandments; this made Isaac and Rebekah sad. Even so, when Isaac became old, he planned to pass the priesthood on to Esau, since Esau was the first-born son. Back in those days, the priesthood wasn't given to

WORD QUEST

- intreated
- barren
- threescore years old
- sod
- pottage

as many people as it is now. It was reserved for a very special few. Esau didn't care much about receiving the priesthood, but Jacob, on the other hand, understood the importance of the priesthood and wanted to receive it so he could bless his family and pass it on to his own children one day.

Before her sons were born, Rebekah had been told by the Lord that Jacob would one day rule over Esau. Rebekay knew that Jacob, not Esau, should receive the priesthood blessing from Isaac. Since Isaac was old and couldn't see very well, Rebekah helped Jacob disguise himself to feel like Esau (who had hairy arms) and to go into Isaac's tent to receive the priesthood blessing. Isaac felt Jacob's arms and believed he was Esau so he gave the priesthood to Jacob. When Esau came later to his father's tent to receive the blessing, he found out that Isaac had given it to Jacob. When Isaac found out he had blessed Jacob instead, he did not take the blessing away or get angry with Jacob; instead he realized that the Lord's will had been done. Even so, this made Esau angry, and he and Jacob became enemies for many years. Rebekah was afraid for Jacob's life so she sent him to live with her brother Laban where Jacob met and married his wife Rachel. Years later, Esau and Jacob met again and Esau forgave Jacob.

VERSES	SUGGESTED QUESTIONS	TREASURES OF KNOWLEDGE
Genesis 25:20–34	• How old was Isaac when he married Rebekah? (v. 20) • What did Isaac pray to the Lord for? Did the Lord give it to him? (v. 21) • What was the Lord's response to Rebekah's concern over her pregnancy? (vv. 22–23) • What were the names of the twins? (vv. 25–26) • Who was born first? (v. 25) • What jobs did Esau and Jacob have when they got older? (v. 27) • What did Esau want Jacob to give him? (v. 30) • What did Jacob ask Esau for in exchange for his pottage? (v. 31) • What was Esau's response to Jacob's request? (vv. 32–33) • When Isaac grew old, it was time to give the priesthood blessing to one of his sons—which son was he planning to bless? (see story) • Who did Rebekah feel should get the priesthood blessing and why? (see story)	**intreated:** prayed to **barren:** could not have children **threescore years old:** three times twenty years old (or sixty years old) **sod:** boiled **pottage:** a thick soup

VERSES	SUGGESTED QUESTIONS	TREASURES OF KNOWLEDGE
Genesis 27:18–29, 41	• When Jacob went into Isaac's tent to receive the blessing, who did he tell his father he was? (v. 19) • Why did Isaac believe that Jacob was Esau? (vv. 22–23) • Name three things that Isaac blesses Jacob with (vv. 28–29) • What was Esau's response when he found out Jacob had received the birthright blessing instead of him? (v. 41) • Where did Jacob go after receiving the blessing? (see story) • Esau was born into the gospel but he didn't think it was very important, and because of that he lost many great blessings. Do you ever feel like Esau? What can you learn from this story about making the gospel a higher priority in your life?	**What blessings were promised to Jacob by his father in Genesis 27:28–29?** He would be able to grow plenty of food; his descendants would be leaders; and those that fought against his family would not win.

LESSON ELEVEN

Joseph Is Sold into Egypt

GOSPEL ART PICTURE KIT

109

STORY

In the last lesson, we learned about Jacob and Esau, the twin sons of Isaac. Jacob received the priesthood from his father, Isaac, which made Esau angry. To avoid Esau, Jacob fled the land and went to live with his uncle, Laban. While living there, Jacob met a girl named Rachel whom he wanted to marry, but Laban told him he must work for seven years before he could marry Rachel. At the end of seven years, Rachel's older sister Leah was still not married, and it was the local custom for the older sister to be married first, so Laban tricked Jacob into marrying Leah by disguising her at the wedding. When Jacob found out, he was angry, so Laban agreed to let Jacob marry Rachel also, as long as he agreed to work another seven years. In Old Testament times, some men had more than one wife, and it was approved of by the Lord.

Jacob's name was later changed by the Lord to Israel, and he went to live in the land of Canaan—the land the Lord had promised to Abraham and his children. Jacob and his wives had twelve sons, and his favorite son was Joseph, the first-born son of Rachel. All the other sons

WORD QUEST
- sheaves
- made obeisance
- vale
- sackcloth
- Pharaoh
- captain of the guard

knew Joseph was favored by their father, and it made them angry. Another reason they hated Joseph was because Jacob had given Joseph a coat of many colors, which represented the birthright blessing.

Joseph was a boy who had many dreams. Two of his dreams were about him one day being a ruler over his brothers. When Joseph told these dreams to his brothers, it made them even angrier. One day, Jacob asked Joseph to go check on his brothers, who were taking care of the animals far away. The brothers had been talking about how angry they were at Joseph and how they wanted to kill him. However, the oldest brother, Reuben, did not want to kill him, and he convinced the others to throw Joseph in a deep pit in the ground when he arrived.

The brothers then noticed a group of men traveling to Egypt and decided to sell Joseph and make some money, but when they weren't watching, another group of men came by, pulled Joseph from the pit, and sold him to the first group. When the brothers returned to the pit, they saw that Joseph was gone. They killed an animal and put its blood on Joseph's coat to look like he had been killed by a wild animal.

When the brothers returned home, they showed Joseph's bloody coat to Jacob and told him Joseph had been killed. Jacob was extremely sad at the loss of his favorite son.

VERSES	SUGGESTED QUESTIONS	TREASURES OF KNOWLEDGE
Genesis 37:1–14	• Where did Jacob live? (v. 1) • Who was his favorite son and why? (v. 3) • What did he give Joseph and what did it represent? (v. 3 and story) • How did Joseph's brothers feel about him being the favorite? (v. 4) • Joseph told his brothers about a dream he had. What was Joseph's dream about? (v. 7) • How did his brothers feel about the dream? (v. 8) • Where did Israel send Joseph? (vv. 13–14)	**Why were Joseph's brothers jealous of the coat of many colors?** Many scholars believe the coat was given to Joseph to symbolize the birthright blessing. The birthright usually went to the first-born son of the first wife, but Reuben, the first-born of Leah, was unfaithful so he could not receive it. The birthright then went to Joseph, the first-born son of Rachel. Joseph was the eleventh of twelve sons, which would explain why the older brothers were jealous of him receiving the birthright blessing.

VERSES	SUGGESTED QUESTIONS	TREASURES OF KNOWLEDGE
Genesis 37:18–36	• What did Joseph's brothers plan to do to Joseph? (vv. 18–20) • What did Reuben (Joseph's oldest brother) want to do to Joseph instead? (vv. 21–22) • What did Judah suggest they do with Joseph? (vv. 26–27) • What did the Midianite merchantmen do with Joseph? (vv. 28) • What did the brothers do with Joseph's coat? (vv. 31–32) • How did Jacob respond to the news about Joseph? (vv. 34–35) • What did the Midianites do with Joseph? (v. 36)	**sheaves:** bundles of wheat **made obeisance:** bowed before a superior **vale:** valley **sackcloth:** rough clothing worn when mourning a loss **Pharaoh:** king of Egypt **captain of the guard:** head of Pharaoh's body guards

LESSON TWELVE

Joseph and Potiphar's Wife

GOSPEL ART PICTURE KIT

418

STORY:

After arriving in Egypt, Joseph was bought by a very powerful man named Potiphar, who served in Pharaoh's army. Even though he had suffered a lot, Joseph continued to have faith and was a righteous man. Potiphar knew that Joseph could be trusted, so after some time, Joseph became the head of all the servants in Potiphar's home. Joseph served Potiphar faithfully and worked hard at his job.

Unfortunately, Potiphar's wife found Joseph attractive and asked him every day to do things with her that only husbands and wives should do with each other, but Joseph refused her. One day when Joseph was alone in the house, Potiphar's wife came to him and asked him to be with her. Joseph knew this was wrong and told her no; he said "how then can I do this great *wickedness*, and *sin* against God?" (Genesis 39:9). Saying no to Potiphar's wife was probably a very difficult thing to do, but Joseph was obedient and didn't want to do anything contrary to God's commandments. Joseph decided the best thing to do was to get far away from the temptation and he fled from the house.

WORD QUEST
- overseer
- wotteth

Potiphar's wife was very angry about being rejected so she lied to get Joseph in trouble. After Joseph fled, she called out to the other servants and told them that Joseph had tried to do things with her that he shouldn't. When her husband came home, she told him the same lie. Because of this, Potiphar put Joseph in prison.

At this point, it would seem normal if Joseph lost his faith in God and thought He didn't love him. But Joseph continued to trust God, and because of this, he was blessed while in prison. The keeper of the guard noticed what a good person Joseph was, and in time Joseph was put in charge of the other prisoners.

VERSES	SUGGESTED QUESTIONS	TREASURES OF KNOWLEDGE
Genesis 39:1–23	• Who bought Joseph from the Ishmaelites? (v. 1) • How did the Lord bless Joseph? (vv. 4–5) • What did Potiphar's wife want from Joseph and how often did she ask him? (vv. 7, 10) • What was Joseph's response to Potiphar's wife? (vv. 8–9) • What happened when Joseph was alone in the house? (v. 12) • What did Joseph do when Potiphar's wife tried to get him to sin? (v. 12) • Have you ever been in a situation where someone wanted you to do something you knew was wrong? If so, what did you do? • What does Joseph's example teach us about what to do when we are tempted? • What lie did Potiphar's wife tell the other servants and her husband when they returned home? (vv. 14–18) • What was Potiphar's response to his wife's lie, and what did he do to Joseph? (vv. 19–20)	**Would you give up your freedom to obey God?** "When Joseph was in Egypt, what came first in his life—God, his job, or Potiphar's wife? Joseph was put in prison because he put God first. If we were faced with a similar choice, where would we place our first loyalty? Can we put God ahead of security, peace, passions, wealth, and the honors of men? When Joseph was forced to choose, he was more anxious to please God than to please his employer's wife. When we are required to choose, are we more anxious to please God than our boss, our teacher, our neighbor, or our date?" (Benson).

VERSES	SUGGESTED QUESTIONS	TREASURES OF KNOWLEDGE
Genesis 39:1–23 (cont.)	• Even though Joseph was put into prison for something he didn't do, tell how the Lord still blessed him. (vv. 21–22) • What responsibility did the keeper of the prison give to Joseph? (v. 22) • How do you think you would feel if you were Joseph and all these bad things kept happening to you? • Would you be able to continue to have faith in the Lord and His love for you? • What does Joseph's example teach you about having faith no matter what?	**overseer:** someone in charge **wotteth:** knoweth

LESSON THIRTEEN

Joseph Interprets Pharaoh's Dreams

STORY

While Joseph was in prison, he correctly interpreted the dreams of two of Pharaoh's servants who were also in prison. Sometime later, Pharaoh had two dreams that bothered him, and none of his magicians or wise men were able to tell him what the dreams meant. It was then that Pharaoh's chief butler, who had been in prison with Joseph, remembered how Joseph had correctly interpreted his dream.

Pharaoh sent for Joseph and explained to him that he had dreamed about seven healthy cows that were eaten by seven sickly cows, and in his second dream, he dreamed about seven healthy ears of corn being blasted away by seven thin ears of corn. The Lord blessed Joseph with the gift of interpreting dreams, and so Joseph was able to explain to Pharaoh that God was giving him a sign of what was about to happen. There would be seven years where lots of food would grow and the animals would be healthy and strong, but then there would be seven years of dryness, where no food would grow and the animals would die. This is called a famine.

WORD QUEST
- kine
- raiment
- arrayed
- vestures
- Zaphnath-paaneah

Joseph recommended that Pharaoh choose a wise man to be in charge of gathering and storing extra food during the years of plenty to feed the people during the years of famine. Pharaoh was so impressed with Joseph that he chose him to be the man in charge. This meant Joseph became the second man in charge of a very large and powerful country—only Pharaoh would have more power. This was a great blessing given to Joseph for all his years of faithfulness and service.

Pharaoh also gave Joseph a wife and they had two sons; Manasseh and Ephraim. Joseph was very happy and helped many people in the land of Egypt during the famine.

VERSES	SUGGESTED QUESTIONS	TREASURES OF KNOWLEDGE
Genesis 41:1–57	• What did Pharaoh dream about? (vv. 1–7) • Who did Pharaoh first ask to interpret his dreams? Were they able to? (v. 8) • Who told Pharaoh about Joseph's ability to interpret dreams? (v. 9) • What did Joseph say to Pharaoh about being able to interpret his dreams? (v. 16) • What did Joseph say was going to happen in the next seven years and then the seven years after that? (vv. 29–30) • How did Pharaoh reward Joseph for his wisdom in being able to interpret his dreams? (vv. 40–42) • Would there be anyone besides Pharaoh who had more power in Egypt than Joseph? (v. 40) • How many sons did Joseph have and what were their names? (vv. 51–52)	**kine:** cow **raiment:** clothing **arrayed:** dressed **vestures:** clothing **Zaphnath-paaneah:** "he who reveals that which is hidden" (see Bible dictionary). The name given to Joseph by Pharaoh.

VERSES	SUGGESTED QUESTIONS	TREASURES OF KNOWLEDGE
Genesis 41:1–57	• Have you ever had a difficult trial where you felt the Lord had forgotten you? If so, what does Joseph's story teach you? • Why do you think the Lord doesn't always immediately bless those who keep His commandments? What would happen if he did? Do you think people would keep the commandments for the right reasons? (see Treasures of Knowledge)	**It took several years before Joseph was blessed for his righteousness. Why do you think the Lord doesn't always immediately bless those who keep His commandments?** " 'If pain and sorrow and total punishment immediately followed the doing of evil, no soul would repeat a misdeed. If joy and peace and rewards were instantaneously given the doer of good, there could be no evil—all would do good and not because of the rightness of doing good. There would be no test of strength, no development of character, no growth of powers, and no free agency. . . . There would also be an absence of joy, success, resurrection, eternal life, and godhood' (Spencer W. Kimball). Our love of God must be pure, without selfish intent. The pure love of Christ must be the motive in our devotion" (Faust).

The Children of Israel Settle in Egypt

GOSPEL ART PICTURE KIT

122

STORY:

The famine that Pharaoh had dreamed about spread to the land of Canaan where Joseph's family lived. When Jacob (Israel), Joseph's father, heard there was food in Egypt, he sent all of his sons except Benjamin, the youngest, to go to Egypt and buy food for the family. Benjamin was the second son of Rachel, and Jacob feared something bad might happen to Benjamin if Jacob let him go.

In Egypt, Joseph was in charge of giving out food to the people who needed it. When his brothers came to buy food, they did not recognize Joseph, but he knew who they were.

When they bowed before Joseph, asking for food, he remembered the dreams he had had about one day being a ruler over his brothers. Joseph asked his brothers if they were spies, but they insisted that they had come from the land of Canaan to buy food for their family. Joseph asked if their father was alive and if they had another brother. They told him how one brother had died and that the other one remained with their father, who was still alive.

WORD QUEST
- earing
- Goshen
- governor
- Rameses

Joseph let them buy food, but he kept one brother in Egypt and told them that if they came back for more food they would have to bring their younger brother with them. Joseph wondered if his brothers were still selfish and jealous like they had been when he was younger, so when they brought Benjamin back the next time to buy food, Joseph decided to test them. Joseph secretly placed an expensive cup in Benjamin's bag of food and then had his servants search all the bags, knowing they would find the cup in Benjamin's bag and take him away to prison. When this happened, Judah, one of the older brothers went to Joseph's house and begged him to release Benjamin; he told Joseph how horrible it would be for their father if something happened to Benjamin. Judah told Joseph he would take Benjamin's place and be Joseph's servant. Joseph then knew that his brothers had changed, so he told them who he was. They were very surprised and happy to find out that Joseph was still alive and grateful that he had forgiven them. Joseph explained that God had changed his unfortunate experience of being sold as a slave into a good thing—a way of saving his family from starving to death during the famine.

Joseph's brothers returned home and brought Jacob and all their families back to Egypt to live. Pharaoh gave their families the land of Goshen to settle in and raise their families. Jacob lived seventeen years in Egypt before he died, and when he died he asked Joseph to bury him where his father and grandfather (Abraham and Isaac) were buried.

VERSES	SUGGESTED QUESTIONS	TREASURES OF KNOWLEDGE
Genesis 42:1–16	• Why did Joseph's brothers come to Egypt? (v. 3) • Which brother did not go to Egypt and why? (v. 4) • Where did Joseph see his brothers again? Did they recognize him? (vv. 6–7) • How did Joseph's earlier dreams come true? (vv. 6, 9) • What did Joseph tell his brothers they needed to do if they wanted to buy more food? (vv. 15–16)	

VERSES	SUGGESTED QUESTIONS	TREASURES OF KNOWLEDGE
Genesis 44:1–2, 11–12, 18, 33–34	How did Joseph test his brothers to see if they had changed? (vv. 1–2) How did the brothers pass the test? (vv. 18, 33–34)	**governor:** ruler
Genesis 45:1–15, 24–30	• Summarize what Joseph said when he revealed himself to his brothers. (vv. 1–15) • Do you think you could forgive someone if they hurt you like Joseph's family hurt him? • What does this story teach you about forgiving others? • Even though it was Joseph's brothers who sent Joseph to Egypt, the Lord used what happened to him to bless his life and his family. How did Joseph's being in Egypt bless his family? (vv. 5–8) • How many years of famine were left at the time Joseph's family came to him? (v. 11) • What was Jacob's reaction when he heard Joseph was alive? (v. 26) • How do you think you would feel if you found out someone you thought was dead was really alive?	**earing:** part of a plant that contains the grain **Joseph's lineage in the latter-days:** Joseph was given the opportunity to bless and save his family from the famine. Many members of the Church are from the lineage of Joseph and are given the responsibility of saving the house of Israel spiritually in the latter days by spreading the gospel across the world.

VERSES	SUGGESTED QUESTIONS	TREASURES OF KNOWLEDGE
Genesis 47:11–12, 27–30	• Where did Joseph's father, brothers, and their families go to live? (v. 11) • How many years did Jacob live in Egypt, and how old was he when he died? (v. 28) • Where did Jacob want to be buried when he died? Who are his "fathers?" (v. 30)	**Goshen:** a land east of the Nile in Egypt **Rameses:** "An Egyptian treasure-city, and also the name of the district surrounding it" (see Bible dictionary).

LESSON FIFTEEN

Moses

GOSPEL ART PICTURE KIT

106

STORY:

The children of Israel lived in Egypt for many years. Eventually Joseph and all his brothers died, but their children and grandchildren grew and had more children. The Pharaoh who knew and loved Joseph also died and a new Pharaoh who did not know Joseph began to be afraid that the children of Israel might one day join with Egypt's enemies and fight against Egypt. This Pharaoh decided to make the Israelites slaves and make them build buildings and cities for him. He also commanded his soldiers to kill every baby boy that was born, so there wouldn't be so many Israelites.

One of the Israelite women had a baby boy whom she hid from the soldiers for three months. When she began to fear he would be found and killed, she put the baby in a basket and placed him in the river. The baby's older sister, Miriam, watched over him and followed the basket in the river. The basket floated to an Egyptian princess who was bathing in the river. When she found the baby, the princess had compassion on him and desired to raise him as her son. Moses's sister told the

WORD QUEST

- grieved
- rigour
- ark of bulrushes
- flags
- nurse
- Midian
- sighed by reason
- groaning

princess she knew of a woman who could help raise the baby and she brought her mother to the princess to help take care of him. The princess named the baby Moses, and when he grew older, he was raised in the palace as an Egyptian prince.

When Moses grew up, he saw the way his people, the Israelites, were treated, and he felt sad. One day, he saw an Egyptian hitting an Israelite man. Later, when he was alone, Moses killed the Egyptian and hid him in the sand. But when the Pharaoh found out about this, he threatened to kill Moses, so Moses fled from Egypt and went far away to a land called Midian.

In Midian, Moses met a man named Jethro who had seven daughters. Moses helped save his daughters from some men who were trying to steal their sheep. Jethro was grateful to Moses and allowed him to live with his family and marry one of his daughters. While living there, Moses learned about the gospel of Jesus Christ and received the priesthood from Jethro (see D&C 84:6).

During this time, the children of Israel were still in bondage to the Egyptians and prayed to God that He would free them. God heard their prayers and remembered the covenant He had made with their fathers—Abraham, Isaac, and Jacob—the covenant that they would inherit the land of Canaan to live freely in. Even though Moses didn't know it, God was preparing him to help free the Israelites and take them to their promised land.

VERSES	SUGGESTED QUESTIONS	TREASURES OF KNOWLEDGE
Exodus 1:7–13, 22	• Did the new Pharaoh of Egypt remember who Joseph was? (v. 8) • What was the Pharaoh of Egypt afraid of? (vv. 9–10) • What did the Pharaoh do to the Israelites? (vv. 11, 13) • What did the children of Israel build for Pharaoh? (v. 11) • What did Pharaoh command his people to do to the Israelite babies? (v. 22)	**grieved:** afraid of their large numbers **rigour:** they were treated cruelly

VERSES	SUGGESTED QUESTIONS	TREASURES OF KNOWLEDGE
Exodus 2:1–25	• What house were Moses's parents from (which of Joseph's brothers did they come from)? (v. 1) • How long was Moses's mother able to hide him? (v. 2) • What did Moses's mother do with him when she could no longer hide him? (v. 3) • Who watched over baby Moses after he was placed in the river? (v. 4) • Who found the baby? (v. 5) • Did she know that he was not an Egyptian baby? (v. 6) • Why do you think she kept the baby even though Pharaoh had commanded all male babies to be killed? • What did Moses's sister say to Pharaoh's daughter? (v. 7) • How was Moses's mother able to take care of Moses while he was still a baby? (v. 9) • Where did Moses's name come from? (v. 10) • What did Moses do to an Egyptian and why? (vv. 11–12) • What happened when the Pharaoh heard about Moses killing the Egyptian? (v. 15) • Where did Moses go? (v. 15)	**ark of bulrushes:** a waterproof basket made from plants **flags:** plants growing in the river **nurse:** feed and take care of **Midian:** Jethro was a descendant of Midian, a son of Abraham; this is why he had the priesthood. **sighed by reason:** felt sad because **groaning:** a sound expressing feelings

VERSES	SUGGESTED QUESTIONS	TREASURES OF KNOWLEDGE
Exodus 2:1–25	• What happened to the Pharaoh? (v. 23) • Did God hear the children of Israel when they cried to Him about being in bondage? (v. 24) • Do you remember what covenant God made with Abraham, Isaac, and Jacob? (Their descendants would be given the gospel and allowed to live freely in the land of Canaan). • Name some ways that the Lord prepared and protected Moses for his mission in life, which was to free the Israelites and give them the gospel of Jesus Christ.	**What's the difference between a Hebrew, an Israelite, and a Jew?** A Jew is both an Israelite and a Hebrew. But not all Israelites are Jews since Israelites come from the twelve sons of Israel and the Jews are descendants from just one son—Judah. Hebrews are any descendants of Abraham, including the Israelites, and therefore the Jews.

LESSON SIXTEEN

Moses Delivers the Israelites

GOSPEL ART PICTURE KIT:
107, 108

STORY

While living in the land of Midian, Moses helped take care of the sheep in the mountains. One day, the Lord came to visit Moses and told him he was to help lead the Israelites from the Egyptians. The Lord appeared to Moses in a burning bush, and at first Moses was afraid, but the Lord told him not to be, and that He would be with Moses and help him. The Lord told Moses that his brother Aaron, who was still in Egypt, would help speak for him since Moses had a speech problem. The Lord gave Moses a large stick, called a staff. He showed Moses how to turn the staff into a snake and told Moses to show this to Pharaoh to convince him that God wanted His people to be free to leave and live in the land of Canaan. God wanted His people to learn to worship Him properly because, while living in Egypt, many of the Israelites had taken on the religious beliefs and practices of the Egyptians, which were not correct.

When Moses and Aaron appeared before Pharaoh and showed him the miracle of the staff turning into a

WORD QUEST
- Horeb
- wonders
- sorcerers

snake, he was not impressed since he had magicians that could do the same thing. The Pharaoh told Moses he would not free the Israelites. Because of the Pharaoh's hard heart, the Lord commanded Moses to turn the river into blood, but once again, the magicians were able to do the same thing, so Pharaoh did not believe it came from God.

Next, the Lord sent thousands of frogs, lice, and flies to all the Egyptians—the pests were in their homes, in their food, and in their water. But still, the Pharaoh would not let the Israelites go free. Because of the Pharaoh's unwillingness to listen, the Lord then caused all of the cattle of the Egyptians to die. Still, Pharaoh refused to free the Israelites. The Egyptians were then afflicted with large sores and blisters on their bodies. After that didn't work, hail and fire fell from the sky, which destroyed their growing food and animals. Yet even after all of this pain and destruction, Pharaoh still said no.

Because of Pharaoh's hard heart and his refusal to listen to the Lord, a plague of grasshoppers came upon the Egyptians and destroyed the rest of their trees and plants. The grasshoppers filled the homes of the Egyptians. But Pharaoh again rejected Moses's request, and so there were three days of darkness where no lights could shine except for in the homes of the Israelites. After that, Pharaoh told Moses that the Israelites could go free but that they must leave all their animals behind. Moses knew they would need their animals to live on and to offer sacrifices to the Lord, so he said they must go and take their animals with them, but Pharaoh said no and that they all must remain.

Finally the Lord told Moses that after one more plague, Pharaoh would let the Israelites go. He told Moses to have all of the Israelites put animal blood on their doors as a sign that they worshipped God. The next night, the first-born sons in all the land died, except for those whose houses had blood over the door. This event is still remembered by the children of Israel today as Passover. It is called this because death "passed over" their houses. When Pharaoh's son died, he was so upset that he agreed to let the Israelites leave Egypt. The children of Israel packed up all their belongings and began the long trek through the wilderness toward the promised land of Canaan.

VERSES	SUGGESTED QUESTIONS	TREASURES OF KNOWLEDGE
Exodus 3:1–12, 19–20 **Exodus 4:1–5** **Exodus 7:8–14, 17, 18** **Exodus 8:1–4, 15–17, 20–21, 32** **Exodus 9:1–9, 22–26, 35** **Exodus 10:12–15, 21–23** **Exodus 11:4–6** **Exodus 12:20–33, 51**	• What was Moses's job in Midian? (Exodus 3:1) • Who appeared to Moses? (Exodus 3:2) • What did the Lord ask Moses to remove and why? (Exodus 3:5) • What did the Lord want Moses to go and do? (Exodus 3:10) • How did Moses feel about the Lord's request? (Exodus 3:11) • Did the Lord promise to be with Moses in helping him deliver the children of Israel? (Exodus 3:12) • Do you think God always helps us when He asks us to do something? If so, how does that make you feel? • What was God's warning to Moses? (Exodus 3:19) • What was God's plan? (Exodus 3:20) • Name five of the plagues that the Lord sent to Egypt. (Look in Exodus 7, 8, 9, 10, 11, and 12.) • What was the last plague and why do you think Pharaoh finally let the Israelites go? (Exodus 12:29–31) • What is Passover and why do you think it is still remembered by Jews today? (see story)	**"the Lord hardened Pharaoh's heart":** It is very important to note that the Lord did not harden Pharaoh's heart; Pharaoh hardened his own heart. The Lord does not control our hearts and our actions—we do. (see JST Ex. 4:21) **Horeb:** "another name for Sinai" (see Bible dictionary) **wonders:** miracles **sorcerers:** people who perform magic by the power of the devil **Why were Pharaoh's magicians able to perform the same miracles?** Satan has power—not the same power as God—but he still has power and he gives it to people to help trick others into following him and not God (see Revelation 16:14) **How can you tell the difference between God's power and Satan's power?** Moroni teaches us that all things that come from God lead us to be good and to believe in Jesus Christ. Anything that leads us away from Jesus, or teaches us to doubt him, is from Satan. (See Moroni 7:12–17)

LESSON SEVENTEEN

Miracles in the Wilderness

STORY

After the Israelites left Egypt, Pharaoh was angry that he had let them go. He decided he wanted to go after them, so he took his soldiers and followed the Israelites into the wilderness.

The Israelites became very frightened when they found out Pharaoh's army was coming after them. When they reached a large body of water called the Red Sea, they became angry with Moses, saying that it would have been better to have remained slaves in Egypt rather than to be killed in the wilderness. Moses prayed to the Lord for help and was told to raise his staff above his head. He was told that the waters of the Red Sea would spread apart so the Israelites could cross on dry land. The Lord held Pharaoh's armies back until the Israelites could safely cross. When the armies began to pursue the Israelites by following them on the dry path, Moses raised his staff from the other side, and the water filled back in and drowned Pharaoh and his armies. The children of Israel were finally free from the Egyptians forever.

However, travelling in the wilderness was not easy, since it was a dry place with very little food and water. The Israelites complained to Moses that at least in Egypt there had been food to eat. Moses prayed, and the Lord

WORD QUEST
- murmur
- manna
- chide

blessed the people with large amounts of birds called quail to eat in the evening; also, every morning, manna appeared on the ground to eat. There was only enough manna for everyone to gather for one day and no more.

Another miracle occurred when the Israelites had no water and were again complaining to Moses. Once again, the Lord blessed them. He told Moses to hit a rock with his staff, and water came pouring out—enough for everyone. These miracles helped the Israelites learn to have faith and to trust that the Lord would provide for their needs each day.

VERSES	SUGGESTED QUESTIONS	TREASURES OF KNOWLEDGE
Exodus 14: 5–16, 21–31	• What did the Pharaoh do after the Israelites left Egypt? (vv. 5–9) • How did the Israelites feel when they saw the armies coming? What did they say to Moses? (vv. 10–12) • What did the Lord tell Moses to do? (v. 16) • How did the Israelites get across the Red Sea? (vv. 21–22) • What happened to the Egyptians who followed after the Israelites? (vv. 27–28) • How did the Israelites feel after witnessing this miracle? (vv. 30–31)	**"went out with a high hand":** an act of showing his defiance
Exodus 16:1–4, 11–15	• Why did the children of Israel murmur in the wilderness? (vv. 2–3) • What miracle did the Lord perform for the Israelites when they were hungry? (vv. 13–14)	**murmur:** complain **manna:** the Hebrew translation means "what is it?" This shows that the Israelites had never seen it before. It tasted sweet, and they used it to make breadlike foods.

VERSES	SUGGESTED QUESTIONS	TREASURES OF KNOWLEDGE
Exodus 17:1–6	• What did the Lord have Moses do for them when they were thirsty? (v. 6) • Why do you think the Israelites continued to murmur and worry about things after all the Lord had done for them? • Do you ever find yourself murmuring when life gets hard? If so, what might be a better way to respond to your trials? • Do you ever doubt that the Lord can help you? • What lesson can you learn from these stories about the love and kindness of God?	**chide:** to express disapproval **miraculous symbols:** "Paul taught that the passage through the Red Sea and the overshadowing of the pillar of fire were clearly types, or symbols, of the baptism of water and fire (See 1 Corinthians 10:1–4)" (Church Educational System, vol. 1 p. 121).

LESSON EIGHTEEN

The Ten Commandments

STORY

When the children of Israel reached the wilderness of Sinai where the Lord had told Moses to bring them, they stopped and made camp. While they were there, the Lord commanded Moses to come to the top of the mountain so he could receive the commandments the Lord wanted Israel to keep. The Lord wanted to make a covenant with the children of Israel that if they kept His commandments, the Lord would bless them and they would be a holy nation.

While Moses was on the mountain, the Lord wrote with His finger the commandments that He wanted the people to keep. While Moses was with the Lord, the people down below became worried because Moses was gone for so long. They wanted a god to worship, and in Egypt they had been taught to make gods out of stone. So the children of Israel gathered all their gold and made a golden calf to worship and make sacrifices to.

The Lord told Moses what was happening to the people and told him to go back. When Moses came down from the mountain and saw what they were doing, he was angry because worshipping anything

WORD QUEST

- peculiar
- graven image
- jealous God
- vain
- hallowed
- false witness
- covet
- guiltless
- burnt offerings and peace offerings
- hew
- wist

besides God is a sin. Moses knew the people were not ready to keep God's commandments, so he threw the tablets on the ground and they broke.

Moses prayed to God, asking Him to forgive the Israelites. The Lord told Moses to make more tablets and to come back up to the mountain where he would give simpler commandments for the Israelites to keep. These are the commandments the Lord told Moses to write:

1. Thou shalt have no other gods before me.
2. Thou shalt not make unto thee any graven image.
3. Thou shalt not take the name of the Lord thy God in vain.
4. Remember the Sabbath day, to keep it holy.
5. Honor thy father and thy mother.
6. Thou shalt not kill.
7. Thou shalt not commit adultery.
8. Thou shalt not steal.
9. Thou shalt not bear false witness against thy neighbor.
10. Thou shalt not covet.

VERSES	SUGGESTED QUESTIONS	TREASURES OF KNOWLEDGE
Exodus 19:1–6	• What covenant did the Lord make with the children of Israel? (vv. 5–6) • It is important to remember that God will never break a covenant—only we can. If we choose to not keep our part we will not receive the blessings. What covenants have you made with God? Are you keeping them?	**"bare you on eagle's wings":** lifted them from their enemies **peculiar:** special 

VERSES	SUGGESTED QUESTIONS	TREASURES OF KNOWLEDGE
Exodus 20:1–17	• Name the Ten Commandments the Lord gave to Moses. (vv. 3–17) • Pick five of the commandments and explain how keeping them can help you be a better person. • Are there any commandments you are having difficulty keeping? If so, how can you do better?	**graven image:** a carved or sculpted object **jealous God:** "possessing sensitive and deep feelings" (see Bible dictionary). God does not want us to worship Him for His sake. He wants us to worship Him because following His plan is the only way to return to live with Him one day. He loves us and wants us to experience the most joy we can have. **vain:** to speak irreverently **hallowed:** to make something holy **false witness:** to lie **covet:** to want something that is not yours **guiltless:** free from guilt **burnt offerings and peace offerings:** "counterfeits of the offerings used to worship the true God" (Ridges, vol. 2, p. 112).

VERSES	SUGGESTED QUESTIONS	TREASURES OF KNOWLEDGE
Exodus 32:1–7, 15–16, 19	• What did the people do when Moses didn't return right away? (v. 1) • What did they make and how did they make it? (vv. 2–4) • What did the people do after building the golden calf? (vv. 5–6) • How did Moses know what was happening to the people while he was on the mountain? (v. 7) • What did Moses bring down with him from the mountain? (vv. 15–16) • What did Moses do when he saw the people worshipping the golden calf? (v. 19)	**hew:** make **wist:** knew **Was the second set of tablets the same as the first set?** The JST for Deuteronomy 10:2 states that the tablets were the same except for the Melchizedek priesthood. "And I will write on the tables the words that were in the first tables which thou brakest, save the words of the everlasting covenant of the holy priesthood, and thou shalt put them in the ark."
Exodus 34:1–5. 28–29	• Did the Lord allow Moses to return to the mountain to receive commandments? (vv. 1–4) • Who wrote the commandments this time? (v. 28) • How long did Moses stay on the mountain without food and water? (v. 28) • Do you know who else in the scriptures went forty days without food and water? (Jesus)	**Why does God give us commandments?** Commandments are given by God to help us attain the greatest amount of peace and happiness, not just in this life, but in the life to come. Commandments show us the best way to act and to treat others so we can ultimately be like our Heavenly Father. He is the only one who knows how to be like Him; His commandments show us the way!

The Children of Israel Wander for Forty Years

STORY

After camping by Mount Sinai, the Lord led the Israelites into the wilderness again toward the promised land of Canaan. When the people were close to Cannan, Moses sent twelve men to spy on the land to see who lived there and what it was like. When the men returned, they reported that it was a beautiful land with plenty of food, but that it was inhabited by a great number of people, too many for the Israelites to fight against and gain the land for themselves.

However, there were two men, Joshua and Caleb, who told Moses and the Israelites that the Lord would help them and that they could fight against the people and live in the land if they trusted in God. But the people did not believe them and were afraid. Again they began to murmur to Moses and wished that they had stayed in Egypt instead of having to fight a battle to win the land.

The Lord was very disappointed in the Israelites' lack of faith. He had shown them miracle after miracle, and yet they still doubted that He could help them obtain the promised land. Because of their complaining and doubts, the Lord told Moses that the Israelites would have to stay in the wilderness for forty years, until all the people who had no faith had died. The Lord promised that Caleb, Joshua, and the younger Israelite children would grow up to possess the promised land.

WORD QUEST
- giants
- rent their clothes
- bade stone them with stones
- carcasses

VERSES	SUGGESTED QUESTIONS	TREASURES OF KNOWLEDGE
Numbers 13:1–3, 17–20, 25–33	• Where did the Lord want the spies to go and search? (v. 2) • What did the Lord want the spies to look for? (vv. 17–20) • How long were the spies gone? (v. 25) • What did the spies say about the land? (vv. 27–28, 31–33)	**giants:** very tall people
Numbers 14:1–11, 26–34	• What did the children of Israel murmur about? (vv. 2–3) • What did Caleb and Joshua say about the land? (vv. 7–9) • What was the Lord's response to the people's complaints? (vv. 27–34) • How long would it be before the Lord would help them get to the land of Canaan? (v. 34) • Who would be allowed to go to the land? (vv. 30–31) • Why did the Lord decide to make them wait so long to obtain the promised land? (see story) • Has the Lord ever asked you to do something that seemed impossible? If so, how did you respond? • What does this story teach you about having continual faith in the Lord?	**rent their clothes:** tore their clothes as a sign of sadness **"bade stone them with stones":** the people were so angry they wanted to stone them. **carcasses:** the body of a dead animal

LESSON TWENTY

Joshua

STORY:

After Moses died, the Lord called Joshua to be the next prophet and leader of the Israelites. It had been forty years since they had gone to spy on the land of Canaan, and now it was time to go and posses the land for themselves. The Lord told Joshua that as long as the people remembered God and kept His commandments, He would watch over them and they would live peaceably in the land.

When they reached Canaan, the cities were filled with people and surrounded by walls that made them seem impossible to conquer, but an angel of the Lord appeared to Joshua and told him that he would receive heavenly help in fighting against the inhabitants of the land. Joshua was told to have his soldiers march around the city walls of Jericho once a day for six days. He was also told to have seven priests blow their horns each time the army marched around the walls. On the seventh day, the armies marched around the walls seven times and the priests blew their trumpets and all the people shouted with a great shout and the walls of the city tumbled down. The Israelite armies were then able to go in and capture the city for themselves.

WORD QUEST

- prosper
- whithersoever
- adversaries
- compass
- noised

After the Lord helped Joshua and the people obtain the land, they divided it up into different parts. Each part belonged to a different "tribe" or "house," which signified which of the twelve sons of Israel they came from. Joshua also taught the people that they must obey God, keep His commandments and serve him. He reminded them that they would only be protected from their enemies and allowed to live in the beautiful land as long as they were righteous.

VERSES	SUGGESTED QUESTIONS	TREASURES OF KNOWLEDGE
Joshua 1:1–7	• Who became the next leader or prophet of Israel after Moses died? (vv. 1–2) • What did the Lord command Joshua to do? (vv. 2, 6) • What did the people need to do if they wanted to prosper in the new land? (v. 7)	**prosper:** to have all the things that you need (food, land, homes, and so forth) and to be protected from enemies **whithersoever:** wherever
Joshua 5:13–15	• Joshua saw a man with a sword; who was he and why was he there? (vv. 14–15 and Treasures of Knowledge)	**adversaries:** someone who fights against you **Who was the "host of the Lord" who appeared to Joshua?** It is not known who appeared to Joshua to give him support before the battle, but some scholars speculate that it could have been Jesus Christ since Joshua was allowed to bow down and worship Him and because Joshua was told he was standing on holy ground.

VERSES	SUGGESTED QUESTIONS	TREASURES OF KNOWLEDGE
Joshua 6:1–5, 20–21, 27	• What did the Lord tell Joshua and his armies to do when they got to the city of Jericho? (vv. 3–5) • What happened to the walls around Jericho? (v. 20) • How did Joshua divide the land up? (see story) • What did the people need to do to be protected from their enemies? (see story) • What promise did the Lord keep to the Israelites? Summarize how He kept it. • What does this story teach you about believing in God's promises?	**compass:** go around **noised:** spread

LESSON TWENTY-ONE

Ruth

GOSPEL ART PICTURE KIT

124

STORY:

After obtaining the promised land, the people of Israel continued to battle against other countries who wanted their land. Whenever they were living righteously, the Lord protected them. But after Joshua died, many of the later generations stopped keeping God's commandments. When this happened, the Lord's protection left, and the Israelites were overcome by their enemies. Nevertheless, the Lord loved His people and continued to send righteous men to help remind them of what God had done for them and who they needed to serve.

For almost two hundred years, there was no prophet who ruled over all of Israel like Moses and Joshua had; instead each tribe ruled themselves and had judges who helped guide them in their decisions and way of life. During this period of time, there was a famine in the land, which meant it didn't rain and crops didn't grow and the people and animals had very little food to eat. While the famine was going on, there was a man and a woman with three sons who were living in Bethlehem. Because of the famine, they traveled to live in the land of Moab, a non-Israelite land, where there was food to eat.

WORD QUEST
- sojourn
- intreat
- glean
- reapers
- sheaves
- wrought
- kinsman
- begat

Soon after arriving in Moab, the man died and the sons married women from Moab who did not worship God. The woman's name was Naomi and her daughter-in-law's were Ruth and Orpah. Naomi, her sons, and her daughters-in-law lived in Moab for ten years before both of her sons died. By this time, Naomi had heard that the famine was over in her land, so she decided to return to Bethlehem. Naomi told her daughters-in-law that they could return to their own families and did not need to go with her to an unknown land with people who lived differently from them. Orpah decided to stay with her family in Moab, but Ruth told Naomi that she wanted to go with her, and that she would worship Naomi's God.

After arriving in Bethlehem, Ruth and Naomi were poor, so Ruth went to the fields close by to glean wheat. This meant that she would gather the extra wheat that had fallen to the ground after the workers had cut the wheat and bundled it up. A righteous man named Boaz owned the wheat fields where Ruth gleaned the wheat. He saw what a kind woman she was for helping Naomi and told his workers to let Ruth gather as much wheat as she needed.

Ruth soon learned that Boaz was a distant relative to Naomi, which meant he would be responsible for marrying Ruth and taking care of her. This pleased Ruth, and soon after, Boaz and Ruth married and had a son named Obed. Obed was the grandfather to David, the king that later united the houses of Israel. The Savior Jesus Christ also descended from Obed.

VERSES	SUGGESTED QUESTIONS	TREASURES OF KNOWLEDGE
Ruth 1:1–8, 14–16, 22	• Why did Naomi and her husband leave Bethlehem to go to Moab? (v. 1) • What was different about Moab? (see story) • What happened to Naomi's husband? (v. 3) • Who did Naomi's sons marry, and how were they different? (v. 4 and story) • How long did Naomi live in Moab? (v. 4) • What happened to Naomi's sons? (v. 5) • Why did Naomi decide to go back to Bethlehem? (v. 6) • Who went with Naomi back to Bethlehem? (v. 16) • Why was it a sacrifice for Ruth to go with Naomi? (v. 16 and story)	**sojourn:** to stay somewhere temporarily **intreat:** plead with

VERSES	SUGGESTED QUESTIONS	TREASURES OF KNOWLEDGE
Ruth 2:1–2, 5–6, 14–16, 18–20	• Where did Ruth gather wheat? (v. 1) • Why did Boaz marry Ruth? (see story)	**glean:** to gather wheat that has fallen from the bundles **reapers:** those who gather and bundle the wheat **sheaves:** bundles of wheat **wrought:** worked **next kinsmen:** closest relative. In those days, the closest male relative could marry a widow, purchase her land, and take care of the family.
Ruth 4:13, 22	• What two important people descended from Ruth and Boaz? (v. 22 and story) • How did the Lord bless Ruth for her loyalty and kindness to Naomi?	**begat:** had a child

LESSON TWENTY-TWO

Samuel

GOSPEL ART PICTURE KIT

111

STORY:

During the period of the Judges when there was no prophet or king to lead all of Israel, a woman named Hannah went to the temple of the Lord and prayed to have a child. She had tried for many years to have a child, but had not been blessed with one. She wanted a child so much that she told the Lord that if He gave her a son, she would allow him to be raised and taught in the temple—she would give his life to the Lord. While praying at the temple, she met a priest named Eli. When Hannah explained to Eli why she was so sad and what she was praying for, he told her to go home and that the Lord would bless her with a child. Hannah believed Eli and stopped being sad. She had hope and faith that her prayers would be answered.

Soon afterwards, Hannah gave birth to a son named Samuel. When he was old enough to be without his mother, he was taken to the temple to be raised by Eli, the priest. The Lord was so pleased with Hannah's faithfulness and sacrifice that he later blessed her with three more sons and two daughters.

WORD QUEST

- Shiloh
- bitterness
- razor come upon his head
- marked
- Belial
- bullocks
- ephah
- ephod
- kick ye at my sacrifice
- cut off thy arm
- open vision

Samuel was a good boy who loved and served the Lord. Eli was also a good man, but two of his sons were not righteous and broke God's commandments. One day, a holy man came to Eli and told him that his sons were wicked and that if Eli did not stop their wicked behavior, he would lose his priesthood power, and it would be given to someone else. Men who hold the priesthood can have it taken from them by the Lord if they are not righteous (see D&C 121:36–37). Even though Eli had been warned, he did not stop his son's wicked behavior in the temple.

One night, while Samuel was sleeping he heard someone call his name and thought it was Eli. He went to Eli's room to ask him what he wanted, but Eli told Samuel that he hadn't called out to him and to go back to bed. This happened two more times. By the third time, Eli realized it was the Lord speaking to Samuel. He told Samuel to go back to his room and to say to the Lord: "Speak Lord, for thy servant heareth" (1 Samuel 3:9). When the Lord spoke to Samuel, one of the things He told him was that Eli and his sons would lose their priesthood power and would die because they had not repented. In the morning, Eli asked Samuel to tell him what the Lord said, and Samuel told him about the Lord's warning. Eli knew the Lord was speaking to Samuel and told him so. Sadly, a short time later Eli and his sons did die.

Samuel later grew to be the prophet of Israel. Israel had not had a prophet to lead them for two hundred years. Samuel was a great prophet whom the people respected. Samuel taught the Israelites to give up their wicked practices and to worship the God who had brought them out of Egypt. The Israelites repented and began to follow the Lord once again.

VERSES	SUGGESTED QUESTIONS	TREASURES OF KNOWLEDGE
I Sam. 1:1–2, 9–20, 24–28	• What was the name of Samuel's mother? (v. 2) • Why did Hannah go to the temple to pray? (v. 11) • What did Hannah promise the Lord if He would answer her prayer? (v. 11) • What did Eli the priest promise Hannah? (v. 17) • How did Hannah's attitude change after speaking to Eli? (v. 18) • Do you think Hannah had a lot of faith in God and in His servant's promise? • What did Hannah name her son? (v. 20) • What did Hannah do with Samuel when he was older? (vv. 26–28) • Would you be willing to make the same sacrifice as Hannah?	**Shiloh:** the religious center of Israel. This is the place where the tabernacle was located (see Bible dictionary). **bitterness of soul:** very sad **What does "razor come upon his head" mean?** He would become a "Nazarite" or a "consecrated man" who did not cut his hair (see Bible dictionary: "Nazarite"). **marked:** saw her mouth moving **daughter of Belial:** Hannah is telling him to not think she is wicked. **bullock:** a young bull **ephah:** a unit of measurement
I Sam. 2:20–21, 26–31	• How did the Lord bless Hannah for her faithfulness? (v. 21) • What did the holy man who came to visit Eli say would happen if his sons did not repent? (v. 31) • Did Eli listen to the man's warning? (see story)	**ephod:** clothing worn by the high priest **kick ye at my sacrifice:** to not take the sacrifices seriously. Eli's sons were stealing from the sacrifices people brought in. **cut off thy arm:** take away his power and authority

VERSES	SUGGESTED QUESTIONS	TREASURES OF KNOWLEDGE
1 Sam. 3:1–21	• Who spoke to Samuel during the night and what did He say? (vv. 8–14) • What does the voice of the Lord sound like to you? Would you know if He was talking to you? • What can you do to help you learn to recognize the Lord's voice? • What happened to Eli and his sons? (see story) • What happens to someone with the priesthood when they become wicked? (see story) • Why do you think it's important for priesthood leaders to be righteous men? • What did Samuel grow up to become? How did he help the Israelites? (see story) • In this story, who listened to God's servant and was blessed? Who did not listen, and what happened to them?	**What was Eli being warned about by the man of God? (1 Samuel 2: 27–31)** The Lord, through a holy man, explained to Eli that the office of the priesthood was given to his ancestors after being freed from Egypt. He also explained that Eli's calling was sacred and not to be taken lightly; it was a job of service, not a way to make money by stealing from the sacrifices people brought to the temple. In these verses, Eli is being warned that his power and his priesthood will be taken away if his sons do not repent. **open vision:** revelations from God **"let none of his words fall to the ground":** all that he prophesied came true

LESSON TWENTY-THREE

David and Goliath

GOSPEL ART PICTURE KIT

112

STORY:

While Samuel was the prophet of Israel, the Israelites asked him to choose a king to rule over them. Samuel warned them that it was not good to be ruled by a king and that they should let God lead them. But the people insisted on having a king, so the Lord told Samuel to appoint a man named Saul to be the king of Israel. At first, Saul was a righteous king who followed the Lord and listened to the counsel of Samuel. But eventually he began to be proud and stopped asking Samuel and the Lord for counsel. Saul felt that he could make his own decisions for the kingdom of Israel.

Because of Saul's unrighteousness, the Lord told Samuel that he needed to choose a new king to lead Israel in the future. Samuel was told to go to Bethlehem where a man named Jesse and his eight sons lived; there he would find the future king. When Samuel met the oldest son, Samuel thought that he looked like he would be a

When a difficult problem lies before you, do you rely on your own strength, or do you trust in the Lord to help you?

WORD QUEST

- sanctify your-selves
- ruddy
- Ramah
- array
- cubit
- mail
- shekels
- greaves
- scrip

good king. But the Lord told Samuel that the boy was not His choice and that He, the Lord, did not look on the outward appearance of a person to know if someone was good, but instead He judged them by their heart.

Samuel then met six more of Jesse's sons, but the Lord told him that none of them were to be the next king. Samuel asked Jesse if he had any other sons. Jesse's youngest son was caring for the flocks in the fields. His name was David. Upon meeting David, the Lord told Samuel that David was to be the next king and to anoint him and bless him as the future king of Israel.

Later on, a battle began between Israel and the Philistines, a group of people that lived close to Israel and who often fought with them for power and control. One of the Philistine soldiers named Goliath was very large and over nine feet tall! The Israelites called him a giant because of his great height. Goliath yelled at the Israelites every day, daring someone to come and fight him but no one would. They were all too afraid. Three of David's older brothers were in the army and David's father sent him to the battle to bring them some food.

When David saw what was happening with Goliath, David went to King Saul and told him that he would fight Goliath. David wondered why the army of Israel was afraid of Goliath. He reminded the king that they were the children of God and that God would help them beat the Philistines. David told Saul how the Lord had helped him fight off a bear and a lion who had tried to kill his sheep once; David knew the Lord would help him defeat Goliath.

King Saul agreed to let David go and fight Goliath, so David collected five smooth stones, took his sling, and went and stood before Goliath. Goliath made fun of David when he saw that a young boy with no armor and no sword had come to stand before him. But David told Goliath he had God with him and that he would kill Goliath and then everyone would know there was a God in Israel and that He protected them; Goliath did not believe David.

When the battle began, David ran toward Goliath, put a stone in his sling, and threw the stone at Goliath's head. The stone hit Goliath in just the right spot to kill him, and he fell to the ground. David then used Goliath's own sword to cut Goliath's head off. When the Philistines saw that Goliath had been slain by David, they ran off and were chased by the Israelite army.

King Saul was so pleased with David's accomplishment that he invited David to come live in the palace and marry one of his daughters.

VERSES	SUGGESTED QUESTIONS	TREASURES OF KNOWLEDGE
I Sam. 16:1, 4–7, 10–13	• What did the Israelites ask Samuel to choose for them? Is this what God wanted for them? (see story) • Who did Samuel choose to be the king? Was this person a righteous man? (see story) • Why did God reject Saul as the king? (see story) • Where did Samuel go to find the future king? (v. 1) • What did Samuel think when he saw Jesse's first son? (v. 6) • How does the Lord judge people? (v. 7) • Why do you think the way we are on the inside is more important than the way we act and look on the outside? • Do you spend more time worrying about how you look and act or arc you more concerned with the thoughts and intents of your heart? • What changes do you need to make on the inside so the Lord will be pleased with you? • Who was chosen to be the next king of Israel? (vv. 11–13)	**sanctify yourselves:** prepare to participate in a sacred act **ruddy:** healthy **withal:** as well as **Ramah:** the town where Samuel lived

VERSES	SUGGESTED QUESTIONS	TREASURES OF KNOWLEDGE
I Sam. 17:1–11, 17, 20–24, 32–37, 40–42, 45–51	• Who was Israel in battle against? (v. 1) • Why was the army of Israel afraid of Goliath? (vv. 4–7) • Why was David not afraid of Goliath? (vv. 34–37) • Do you ever doubt God's ability to help you in a tough situation? • What does David's example teach you about having faith in the Lord's help? • How did David beat Goliath? (vv. 49–51) • What did the Philistines do after they saw David slay Goliath? (vv. 51–52) • What did Saul do for David? (see story)	**array:** order **cubit:** measurement of length **coat of mail:** flexible armor made of rings hooked together **shekels:** Hebrew unit of weight **greaves:** armor for the legs **Why did David call Goliath an "uncircumcised Philistine"?** All Israelite males were circumcised as a sign of the covenant between God and Abraham. Circumcision was also done as a way of separating Israelites from those of the world. **scrip:** bag

LESSON TWENTY-FOUR

King David

STORY

After David defeated Goliath, he became a leader in Saul's army. David was a great leader and helped the Israelites win many battles. The people of Israel loved and admired David, which made King Saul jealous. He became so jealous that he tried several times over the course of many years to kill David. There were many instances when David could have killed Saul, but because of David's respect for the king, he did not kill him. David spent many years in hiding until after Saul's death. Then David returned and became king over Judah, the southern part of Israel. Saul's son became the king over the northern Israelite kingdoms. However, Saul's son was later killed, and the rulers of Israel asked David, who was only thirty years old, to be their king also. David ruled as the king over all of Israel for forty years.

David was a righteous man who loved and served the Lord. However, he later became tempted to sin because of a beautiful woman he saw. This woman, Bathsheba, was married to a leader in David's army whose name was Uriah. While Uriah was away in a battle, David slept with Bathsheba, which is a great sin. David later found out that Bathsheba was pregnant. David knew that he had made a terrible mistake, but instead of repenting and

WORD QUEST
- tabrets
- eyed
- purified
- wayfaring
- blasphemy

asking for forgiveness, he tried to hide his mistake by asking Uriah to come back from the battle to be with his wife. That way everyone would believe the baby was Uriah's. But Uriah was a dedicated soldier who did not want to leave his men behind in battle while he went home. David became more frustrated and upset and told his leaders to place Uriah at the front of the battle, with no protection, so he would be killed.

After Uriah was killed, David married Bathsheba so no one would know of their sin of adultery when she had a baby. After the baby was born, it became very sick and later died.

Nathan, the prophet at that time, came to David and told him that he knew of the sins David had committed. Nathan told him how displeased the Lord was with David. Nathan then explained that David had been given so much from the Lord, and yet he still took something that was not his. David took Uriah's only wife from him and had Uriah killed. David was very sad and felt sorrowful for his sins. He spent many years of his life praying for the Lord's forgiveness. We do not know how the Lord will judge David in the next life, but we do know that the Lord knows David's heart and will judge David fairly for his actions.

VERSES	SUGGESTED QUESTIONS	TREASURES OF KNOWLEDGE
1 Sam. 18:5–9, 12, 28–29; 19:1–2, 18	• What position was David given by Saul? (1 Samuel 18:5) • Why was Saul jealous of David? (1 Samuel 18:6–9) • Why did David have to go into hiding? How long was he in hiding? (1 Samuel 19:1–2, and story) • Even though David had the opportunity to kill Saul, why didn't he? (see story) • What happened to Saul? (see story)	**tabret:** an instrument **eyed:** to watch someone closely
2 Sam. 2:4, 10–11; 5:1–5	• What kingdom did David rule over first? (2 Samuel 2:4) • How old was David when he was anointed king over all of Israel? (2 Samuel 5:4) • How long was David king of Israel? (2 Samuel 5:4)	
2 Sam. 11:2–5, 10–11, 14–15, 26–27	• What sin did David commit first? (vv. 4–5) • What did David do to cover up his sin? (vv. 14–15) • What did David do after Uriah was killed? (vv. 26–27) • Why was the Lord displeased with David?	**purified:** to be clean; usually in regard to a woman's menstrual cycle or after giving birth **wayfaring:** traveling
2 Sam. 12:1–9	• Summarize the parable Nathan tells David and explain how it relates to David's life. (vv. 1–4) • Do you ever want things that aren't yours? • Do you feel that you're grateful for what the Lord has blessed you with or do you seem to always want more?	

VERSES	SUGGESTED QUESTIONS	TREASURES OF KNOWLEDGE
2 Sam. 12:13–19	• What happened to David and Bathsheba's baby? (v. 15) • The story of David and Bathsheba is a sad story, and it shows how even a great servant of the Lord can be tempted by Satan to commit a terrible sin. What should David have done when he first saw Bathsheba? • What other person have we read about who was tempted by a woman but made a different choice than David? (Joseph and Potiphar's wife) • What should David have done after he slept with Bathsheba? • What does this example teach you about admitting your mistakes and being willing to repent of them? • What was the greatest sin David committed? • Have you ever been in a situation when you did something wrong but instead of admitting it you tried to cover it up? • Why is it better to admit your mistakes than lie about them?	**blasphemy:** disrespect for the Lord and His teachings **2 Sam. 12:13—JST: "The Lord hath not put away thy sin that thou shalt not die."** David committed two very serious sins, so much so that he will have to pay the price for the sin of murder himself because it is not covered by the Atonement. Heavenly Father and Jesus will determine David's punishment.

LESSON TWENTY-FIVE

King Solomon

STORY:

King David and his wife Bathsheba later gave birth to another son named Solomon. David taught Solomon to serve the Lord and keep His commandments. When David died, Solomon became the next king of Israel. Solomon prayed and asked the Lord to bless him. Solomon was worried about leading Israel because there were so many people. He wasn't sure how to know right from wrong in the many decisions he needed to make.

The Lord asked Solomon what it was he wanted, and Solomon answered that he wanted to be wise. It pleased the Lord that Solomon did not ask for a long life, or for riches, or to be able to defeat his enemies. Instead, he had asked for an understanding heart. The Lord was so pleased with Solomon's selfless request that He granted the gift of wisdom to him, and He also blessed Solomon with riches and honor, even though Solomon did not ask for them.

Solomon became the wisest king in all the land; he counseled his people with righteous judgment. One example of his wisdom was when two women came to him with a baby. Both of the women had given birth to babies around the same time and lived in the same house. However one of the babies died when his mother

WORD QUEST
- Gibeon
- clave
- concubines

accidently lay on top of him while sleeping. The mother then took her dead baby and switched it with the living baby while the other mother slept. When the second mother rose in the morning and found a dead baby next to her, she knew it was not her baby but the other mother would not admit what she had done and claimed that the living baby was hers.

The two women asked King Solomon to decide who would get the living baby. The real mother of the baby told the story to King Solomon but the other mother lied and said it wasn't true. King Solomon asked that a sword be given to him and told the women he would cut the baby in half and give each woman half of the baby. Of course he would not have killed the baby; he was doing this to find out who the real mother was. The real mother of the baby begged the king not to kill the baby and told him the other mother could have him. But the other mother told him to go ahead and cut the baby in half, then neither of the women would have a baby. King Solomon immediately knew who the real mother was and gave the baby to her.

People from all over the country and surrounding countries heard about the great wisdom of King Solomon and came from far away to receive his wise counsel. King Solomon knew that his father David had wanted to build a great temple to the Lord, but there had been too many wars in the land, and it was not the right time. However, the Lord had told David that his son would build the temple one day. When Solomon became king, he was blessed with peace in the land and knew that it was time to build a temple. Solomon and the people spent seven years building a beautiful temple to worship the Lord in. Solomon counseled his people to be righteous, to worship the Lord, and to repent of their sins.

However, Solomon, like the kings before him, became tempted by Satan and enticed by the things of the world. Solomon began making choices that were contrary to God's commandments. Solomon married women outside of Israel, many of whom worshipped idols, or false gods, which is a sin. Solomon allowed these teachings to be brought into Israel and eventually he began to offer sacrifices to these idols also. When he did this, Solomon lost the help and the spirit of the Lord. Sadly, Solomon did not stay true to the commandments of the Lord throughout his life.

VERSES	SUGGESTED QUESTIONS	TREASURES OF KNOWLEDGE
I Kings 3:3–28	• Who became the king of Israel after David died? (see story) • What did Solomon ask the Lord to bless him with and why? (vv. 7–9) • Why was the Lord pleased with Solomon's request? (vv. 10–11) • What did the Lord bless Solomon with? (vv. 12–14) • Why did the two women with babies come to see King Solomon? (vv. 16–23) • How did Solomon solve this problem? (vv. 24–25) • How did Solomon know who the real mother was? (vv. 26–27) • The mother of the baby who died chose to lie and tried to cover up her accident. How is this story similar to David and Bathsheba? • What is the best thing to do when you make a mistake?	**Gibeon:** "The tabernacle built by Moses was located in Gibeon along with the great altar upon which sacrifices had been offered since the days of Moses" (Church Educational System, vol. 2, p. 4). **Why was Solomon blessed for seeking wisdom?** The prophet Joseph Smith explained "If we seek first the kingdom of God, all good things will be added. So [it was] with Solomon. First he asked wisdom, and God gave it to him—and with it every desire of his heart" (Jackson, 36).
I Kings 5:2–5	• What did King Solomon build for the Lord? (v. 5) • Why was David not able to build a temple? (v. 3) • How long did it take to build the temple? (see story)	

VERSES	SUGGESTED QUESTIONS	TREASURES OF KNOWLEDGE
1 Kings 11:1–6, 9	• What did King Solomon counsel his people to do after the temple was built? (see story) • Did King Solomon keep his own counsel? (v. 4) • What did King Solomon do that was a sin before the Lord? Why do you think doing this is so wrong? • Name one thing each king (Saul, David, and Solomon) did that was wrong. Why do you think the kings committed such great sins? • It seems that Satan knows each of our weaknesses; do you know your weaknesses? • The example of these once great men shows the power of temptation. What can you do to protect yourself from being tempted by Satan	**1 Kings 3:14; 1 Kings 11:4—JST:** The JST corrects the meaning of these verses to show that the Lord was displeased with David's heart and actions. JST 3:14 reads "And if thou wilt walk in my ways to keep my statues, and my commandments, then I will lengthen thy days, and thou shalt not walk in unrighteousness, as did thy father David" (Church Educational System, vol. 2, p. 4). **clave:** became close **concubines:** a secondary wife, usually from a lower class, with fewer privileges than a first wife **What does 1 Kings 11:5 mean?** Ashtoreth and Milcom are names of gods that were worshipped by those outside of Israel. Solomon began to worship these gods and introduced this practice to the Israelites.

LESSON TWENTY-SIX

The Prophet Elijah

STORY

After the death of King Solomon, his son Rehoboam became king. However, Rehoboam told the people he would make them work harder and pay him more taxes. This made several of the tribes angry and they rebelled and anointed their own king, a man named Jeroboam. The Lord allowed this division to happen because of the disobedience of King Solomon in bringing idol worship into the land of Israel. When the twelve tribes of Israel divided, the ten tribes that lived in the northern part of the land followed Jeroboam and became the kingdom of Israel. The remaining two tribes, Judah and Benjamin, stayed with Rehoboam and became the kingdom of Judah. The twelve tribes of Israel were never united again after this division.

During this time, the two kingdoms often fought with one another and neither of the kings were righteous men who followed the prophets and worshipped the Lord. The Lord sent many prophets to warn the kings but the kings did not listen. In fact, the kings often became angry with the prophets; they did not want to be told they were wrong. One of the later kings of Israel named Ahab was so wicked that he "did more to *provoke* the Lord God of Israel

WORD QUEST
- Tishbite
- meal
- cruse
- sojourn

to anger than all the kings of Israel that were before him" (I Kings 16:33).

Ahab was warned by the prophet Elijah to repent and to teach his people to follow God or there would be a great famine in the land. This made Ahab so angry that Elijah was warned by the Lord to hide so Ahab wouldn't have him killed. Elijah hid by a stream of water and the Lord sent ravens with food every morning and every evening to feed him. But soon, the water in the stream dried up because of the famine, so the Lord sent Elijah to a city and told him he would meet a woman there who would feed him.

Upon arriving at the city, Elijah met a widow who was gathering sticks. He asked her to bring him some bread to eat. The widow explained that she only had enough meal and oil to make one last small cake for her and her son before they died. Elijah the prophet promised the woman in the name of the Lord, that if she made him a cake first, then she would have enough meal and oil to make enough food for them until the famine ended. The woman believed the prophet, made him his cake, and the meal and oil sustained them throughout the famine.

After the famine, the woman's son became very sick and died. The woman was extremely sad and asked Elijah why such a horrible thing would happen to her after all the good she had done. Elijah prayed to the Lord and asked for the boy to be healed, to be able to live again with his mother. The Lord heard Elijah's prayer and the boy returned to life. It was a wonderful miracle that showed the woman and all those who heard about it that Elijah truly was a prophet of God, and that the things he taught were true.

VERSES	SUGGESTED QUESTIONS	TREASURES OF KNOWLEDGE
I Kings 17:1–24	• What happened to the twelve tribes of Israel? (see story) • What was the name of each kingdom and which tribes went with each kingdom? (see story) • Who became the king of each kingdom? (see story) • Who was Ahab the king over? Was he a righteous or a wicked king? (see story) • What did Elijah tell Ahab would happen if he didn't repent? (v. 1) • Who told Elijah to go into hiding? (v. 2)	

VERSES	SUGGESTED QUESTIONS	TREASURES OF KNOWLEDGE
I Kings 17:1–24	• How was Elijah able to eat and drink? (v. 4) • Why did Elijah have to go into the city? (vv. 7–8) • Who did the Lord tell Elijah he would meet in the city? (v. 9) • What did Elijah ask the widow to do for him? (v. 11) • What was the widow's response to Elijah's request? (v. 12) • Why do you think Elijah would ask the widow to give him the last of her food? • What did Elijah promise the widow if she fed him? (vv. 13–14) • Why do you think the woman decided to do as Elijah asked? What does her example teach you about following the prophet? • How was the widow blessed for following the prophet? (v. 16) • What happened to the widow's son? (v. 17) • How did Elijah again bless the widow? What miracle did he perform? (vv. 22–23) • Do you ever feel like the things the prophet asks us to do are hard? What lesson can you learn from the story of the widow?	**Tishbite:** the place where Elijah was from **meal:** powder made from grain, like wheat or corn. **cruse:** a pot that holds liquids **sojourn:** a temporary stay **stretched himself upon the child:** blessed him by the power of the priesthood

LESSON TWENTY-SEVEN

Jonah

STORY:

There was a prophet named Jonah who lived in the kingdom of Israel. The Lord told Jonah to go to a land called Nineveh and warn the people that they needed to repent and follow God's commandments or they would be destroyed. The city was full of wicked people who were mean to one another and to people from other countries. Jonah was afraid to go to Nineveh and he also didn't believe they would repent, so he fled in a ship to another country that was far away and in the other direction from Nineveh.

While Jonah was aboard the ship, a great storm arose that threatened to sink the ship. The crew of the ship was frightened and believed it was a sign from God that someone had displeased Him. The crew woke Jonah up from his sleep to ask him what they should do. Jonah told them to throw him off the ship because he knew he was the one the Lord was displeased with.

After he was thrown off the ship, a great fish swallowed Jonah but he was kept alive for three days. Jonah prayed to the Lord and asked for forgiveness for not doing what was asked of him. The Lord gave Jonah another chance, and the fish put him on the shore where he could travel to Nineveh.

WORD QUEST
- Tarshish
- Joppa
- wares
- cast lots
- sackcloth
- gourd

Jonah followed the Lord's command and told the people of Nineveh they needed to stop being wicked and mean or their great city would be destroyed. The people of Nineveh and their king listened to Jonah and repented. Even though the people began to follow God's commandments, Jonah did not believe they should be saved. He could not understand why God would not destroy them because they had been so bad before.

Jonah decided to build a shelter on a hill overlooking Nineveh and wait for the Lord to destroy the city; he was sure that God would. While he was waiting, a plant grew that offered shade to Jonah but it soon died. Jonah was upset when the plant died, and God told Jonah that Jonah cared more about the plant than about the thousands of people in Nineveh who were God's children. God's final words to Jonah were "should not I spare Nineveh?" God loves all of His children and wants them to have the opportunity to repent and receive the gospel, no matter how wicked they have been.

VERSES	SUGGESTED QUESTIONS	TREASURES OF KNOWLEDGE
Jonah 1:1–6, 9–12, 15, 17	• Where did the Lord ask Jonah to go? Why didn't Jonah want to? (v. 2 and story) • Where did Jonah go instead? (v. 3) • What happened while Jonah was on the ship? (v. 4) • What did Jonah tell the sailors to do with him? (v. 12) • What happened to Jonah after he was thrown into the sea? (v. 17) • How long was Jonah in the belly of the great fish? (v. 17)	**Tarshish:** an ancient sea city, possibly in Spain **Joppa:** a sea town in Israel **wares:** merchandise **cast lots:** a way of making a decision like flipping a coin. It was thought to be a way to know the will of God in a situation.

VERSES	SUGGESTED QUESTIONS	TREASURES OF KNOWLEDGE
Jonah 2:1, 10; 3:1–5, 10	• What did the Lord command Jonah to do after being freed from the fish? (Jonah 3:2) • Did the people of Nineveh repent? (Jonah 3:5)	**sackcloth:** clothing worn during a period of sadness **"God repented of the evil":** JST Jonah 3:10 corrects this verse to say that "they turned from their evil way and repented; and God turned away the evil that he had said he would bring upon them." **gourd:** a plant
Jonah 4:1, 11	• How did Jonah feel about the people repenting and why do you think he felt that way? (v. 1) • Do you ever have a hard time forgiving someone when they have done something really mean to you? Do you wish that they would be punished? This might have been how Jonah felt. The people of Nineveh were very mean to the people of Israel. Maybe Jonah had a hard time believing they should be let off the hook after all the bad they had done. What can you learn about forgiveness from the story of Jonah and how can you apply it to your life?	

LESSON TWENTY-EIGHT

Daniel in the Lion's Den

GOSPEL ART PICTURE KIT

117

STORY

The Israelite people went through times of righteousness and peace and periods of disobedience and war. Because they were mostly disobedient, the Lord stopped protecting them, and eventually a country to the north, called Assyria, fought with the Israelites and won. As a result, the Assyrians either killed or captured most of the Israelites (the ten tribes living in the northern part of the land). The Israelites who were captured never returned to their homeland, which is why they are often referred to as the "lost tribes of Israel." They eventually intermarried and lived with people from other countries—they no longer lived in individual tribes—so it is unknown where their descendants are now. It has been prophesied, though, that they will one day be "found," meaning their descendants will be known, and that they will accept the gospel and return to the land of Israel.

Many years after the northern tribes were captured, the Babylonians (a country next to and associated with Assyria) fought with the kingdom of Judah and began

WORD QUEST

- decree
- Medes
- Persians
- altereth not
- signet
- lamentable
- Cyrus the Persian
- Darius

taking children and bringing them to Babylon to live in the king's palace. These children, who were the smartest and the healthiest, were given an education and an opportunity to be a part of the Babylonian government.

Daniel was a young Jewish boy who was taken to Babylon. He was very obedient in keeping God's commandments. He impressed the people who were in charge of him because he had the spirit of the Lord with him, and he soon became a favorite of the king. When he got older, the king desired to place Daniel as second in command in his kingdom. This made many of the other officers to the king very jealous. The officers looked for things that Daniel might be doing wrong, so that they could tell the king and he wouldn't promote Daniel. But they couldn't find anything bad about Daniel's behavior, so instead they devised a plan that would get rid of Daniel and allow one of them to rise to power.

The officers knew that Daniel worshipped and prayed to God every day so they encouraged the king to sign a law stating that "whosoever shall ask a petition of any God or man for thirty days, save [the] king, he shall be *cast* into the den of lions" (Daniel 6:7). The law that the king signed was one that could not be overturned or changed, even by the king himself, no matter what.

Daniel knew about the new law; however, he was not afraid. He knew that praying to God was more important than obeying that law, so he continued to pray three times a day every day. He didn't pray in hiding; he prayed in his house with the windows open, knowing he could be seen. When the officers found Daniel praying, they went to the king, reminded him of his law, and stated that Daniel had been praying. The king was very sad and tried to find a way he could save Daniel, but he knew there was nothing he could do. The king told Daniel to pray to His God, knowing that only God could save him.

Daniel was then thrown into the Lion's den, and the king stayed up all night, praying and worrying about Daniel. In the morning, the king ran to the den and yelled down to Daniel to see if he was still alive. Daniel answered back that he was alive and that the Lord had sent an angel to protect him from the lions. The king was very happy and had Daniel removed from the den. The officers who had tricked the king were then thrown into the den of lions where they were all killed for trying to have Daniel killed. The king also sent a decree among the people that they should recognize Daniel's God as the living God. Daniel was given power and authority and served in the kingdom for many more years.

VERSES	SUGGESTED QUESTIONS	TREASURES OF KNOWLEDGE
Daniel 6:1–28	• What happened to the ten tribes of Israel? (see story) • Why are they referred to as being "lost"? (see story) • What did the Babylonians do with some of the children from Judah? (see story) • Who was Daniel and why was he a favorite of the king? (see story) • What position did King Darius want to promote Daniel to? (v. 2–3) • Do you notice any similarities between Daniel and another person we've studied about in the Bible? (Joseph in Egypt was second in command to Pharaoh) • Explain the law that the officers tricked the king into making. (v. 7) • Why did the officers want to make this law? (vv. 4–5) • What was the punishment for breaking the law? (v. 7) • Did Daniel obey the law? What did he do? (v. 10) • What would you have done if you were Daniel? • What can you learn from Daniel's example about standing up for your beliefs no matter what? • How did the king feel when he found out Daniel had been praying? (v. 14)	**Darius:** The Babylonian king who captured Daniel as a boy died, and his son ruled for many years. Eventually Babylon was captured by another empire, the Persians, and Darius became the king. **decree:** a law **Medes:** people from the ancient country of Media in western Asia **Persians:** people from the ancient empire Persia in western Asia **altereth not:** the law could not be changed by anyone, even the king. **signet:** an official seal made by a ring **lamentable:** sad **Cyrus the Persian:** the king of Persia after King Darius

VERSES	SUGGESTED QUESTIONS	TREASURES OF KNOWLEDGE
Daniel 6:1–28	• What happened to Daniel in the den? (v. 22) • What happened to the officers who tricked the king? (v. 24) • The king sent out a decree to all the people about Daniel's God. What did it say? (vv. 26–27)	

LESSON TWENTY-NINE

Esther

GOSPEL ART PICTURE KIT

125

STORY

In the last story, we learned that some Jewish children were taken to Babylon to be taught in the palace and serve in the government. Eventually though, the Babylonians destroyed Judah and brought most of the Jews to Babylon to live as captives. After many years, the Babylonian empire was taken over by the Persians, and one of their kings, Cyrus, allowed the Jews to return to Jerusalem and rebuild their temple.

However, some of the Jews did not return to Jerusalem but instead remained in Persia. One of these was a girl named Esther who lived with her cousin Mordecai because her parents were dead. The king of Persia needed to find a new queen, so he asked for all the beautiful young women to be brought to the palace so he could choose a new queen from among them. Esther was very beautiful, so Mordecai brought her to the palace. Mordecai told her not to tell anyone she was a Jew. The king loved Esther and chose her to be his queen. So Esther, a young Jewish girl, became Queen of Persia.

WORD QUEST

- virgin
- Vashti
- Shushan
- Tebeth
- Adar
- Scepter

During this time, there was a man named Haman who served as second in command in the kingdom. The king commanded that everyone should bow before Haman when in his presence, but Mordecai would not bow before Haman. This made Haman angry and when he found out Mordecai was a Jew, Haman told the king that there were people in the land that lived by their own laws. Haman told the king that he should protect himself by having them all killed. The king agreed and signed a written agreement that all the Jews would be killed on a certain date.

When Esther heard about the decree, she told Mordecai to have all the Jews fast for her for three days, so she could go to the king and ask him to save the Jews. Esther was afraid because there was a law that no one could approach the king unless he was summoned and Esther had not been called to see the king in thirty days. Anyone who broke the law would be killed unless the king held out his golden scepter. Esther knew that she was taking a great risk in approaching the king, but Mordecai had told her that maybe this was why she had been chosen to be the queen.

At the end of the fast, Esther went to the king. When the king saw her, he held out his golden scepter, and she was allowed to speak to him. Esther invited the king and Haman to a banquet where she told the king she would tell him her request. At the banquet, Esther asked the king to spare her life and her people's lives. The king did not know that Esther was a Jew and that Haman had set up this plot to have them killed. The king was very angry with Haman for tricking him and had Haman hanged. Mordecai was then given Haman's place in the palace, and the king reversed the decree and none of the Jews were killed—Esther the Queen had saved her people.

VERSES	SUGGESTED QUESTIONS	TREASURES OF KNOWLEDGE
Esther 2:2–8, 15–17	• The Jews were taken captive to Babylon for many years. Who eventually allowed them to return to Jerusalem? (see story) • Did all of the Jews return to Jerusalem? (see story) • Did Esther and Moredcai return to Jerusalem or live in Persia? (see story) • What did Esther become? (v. 17) • Did Esther tell anyone she was a Jew? (see story)	**virgin:** an unmarried girl **Vashti:** She was the previous queen but she had disobeyed the king so he sought a new queen. **Shushan:** the capital city **Tebeth:** the fourth month of the Jewish calendar

VERSES	SUGGESTED QUESTIONS	TREASURES OF KNOWLEDGE
Esther 3:1–5, 8, 13–14	• Why was Haman angry with Mordecai? (v. 2) • What did Haman trick the king into signing? (vv. 8, 13) • What other story have we read about where a king was tricked into signing a law against the Jews? How are the stories similar? (Daniel and the lion's den)	**Adar:** the sixth month of the Jewish calendar
Esther 4:5–17; 5:1–4	• What did Esther do when she found out about the decree to kill the Jews? (v. 16) • What does Esther's example teach you about the power of fasting? • Why was it risky for Esther to go see the King? (see story)	**scepter:** a staff held by the king, showing his authority
Esther 7:1–7, 10	• What did the king do when he found out about the law he had signed? (v. 10) • Were the Jews saved? (see story) • Esther lived as a queen in the palace, and no one knew she was a Jew. It would have been very easy for her to not say anything to the king, to not risk her life by going to him and telling him who she was. Why do you think she took such a great risk? • Are you ever afraid to tell people about your beliefs? If so, how can Esther's story help you?	**What can Esther teach us?** "Like Esther, we must prepare for our time because our time has come. We must possess the spiritual strength to overcome our challenges, laying our faults on the altar and giving our lives to the Lord. We must focus our priorities on contributing, as we are able, to the building of the kingdom of God through service" (Smoot 1997).

LESSON THIRTY

Job

STORY

The book of Job is a story about a very righteous, wealthy man who loved the Lord. In the story, we are told that "there was a day when the *sons* of God came to present themselves before the Lord, and *Satan* came also among them to present himself before the Lord" (Job 1:6). On this day, Satan told God that the only reason Job was so good and righteous was because the Lord had blessed him with a large family, lots of friends, and a large amount of land and animals. Satan said that it was easy for Job to love the Lord because the Lord had given him so much. Satan said that if those things were taken away, then Job would curse God instead of worship Him.

Is it hard to have faith and trust in God when bad things happen?

The Lord knew that Job was sincere in his love and righteousness, so he allowed Satan to take away all that Job had, even his health, to prove that he would not curse God, but would still worship and love Him.

WORD QUEST
- eschewed
- Sabeans
- Chaldeans
- rent his mantle
- potsherd
- bemoaned

Soon afterwards, Job lost all of his possessions; he lost his animals, his servants, his house and all ten of his children in one day. Job was very upset and sad about all he had lost, but he did not curse God. Instead he said "the Lord gave, and the Lord hath taken away; blessed be the name of the Lord" (Job 1:21). Job understood that everything he had previously been given was from the Lord and that the Lord could take it all away, since it was His, not Job's.

Satan still believed that if Job were to lose his health, then he would curse God, so Satan was allowed to afflict Job with boils (large, painful sores) over his entire body. But Job did not curse God. Job's wife asked him if he was going to curse God now and give up his faith, but Job told her that he had received all the good God had given him and he would also receive the bad that came to him.

Job's friends accused Job of committing a sin—they said that bad things don't happen to righteous people, but Job explained that often good things happen to the wicked and bad things happen to the righteous, but that the wicked would be judged in the next life.

Even though Job never cursed God or lost his faith, he was still sad and wished he didn't have to go through his trials. He didn't understand why he had to suffer but he trusted that God understood and loved him and knew what was best for him.

Because of Job's great faith, the Lord restored all that Job had lost—He even doubled his land, his animals, and his wealth and blessed him with more children. Job went on to live a long and happy life.

VERSES	SUGGESTED QUESTIONS	TREASURES OF KNOWLEDGE
Job 1:1–3, 6–22	• Name some of the blessings Job had been given? (v. 3) • Why did Satan think Job was so good? (vv. 9–10) • What did Satan think would happen if Job lost everything? (v. 11) • Name four things Job lost in one day. (vv. 14–19)	**escheweth:** keeps away from **Sabeans:** an Arab group from Africa **Chaldeans:** a group of people from Babylon **rent his mantle:** tore his cloak as a sign of mourning

VERSES	SUGGESTED QUESTIONS	TREASURES OF KNOWLEDGE
Job 2:1–10	• What was the next bad thing that happened to Job? (v. 7) • What did Job's wife tell him when he got sick? What was Job's response to her? (v. 9–10) • What do Job's responses teach you about how to respond during difficult times?	**potsherd:** piece of broken pottery
Job 42:10–17	• What did Job's friends say to him? (see story) • If you are righteous does it mean you will never have bad things happen to you? • If you are not righteous can you still have good things in life? Why? • Why do you think the Lord allows bad thing to happen to good people? (see Treasures of Knowledge) • What eventually happened to Job? (vv. 12–17) • Discuss one thing that you learned from this story that you can apply to your life now.	**bemoaned:** to express sadness **Why do bad things happen to good people?** "God does not pamper those he would make strong. According to President Joseph Fielding Smith, 'Tribulation is the heritage of the righteous. It was never intended that those who serve the Lord in faithful obedience to covenants should find a rosy path to eternity. Persecution has been the reward of righteousness'" (Ludlow, 265). The Lord loves us and is testing our faith to see if we will still love Him and worship Him even when life is hard. Our faith and righteousness cannot depend on us having an easy life.

Appendix

Time Line of Major People and Events in the Old Testament

YEAR	EVENT
4000 BC	Adam and Eve
3870 BC	Cain, Abel, Seth (sons of Adam and Eve)
3387 BC	Enoch (great-great-great-grandson of Seth) and the building of Zion
2944 BC	Noah (great-great-grandson of Enoch) and the flood
2452 BC	Shem (son of Noah)
2022 BC	Abraham (seventh great-grandson of Shem)
1922 BC	Isaac (son of Abraham and Sarah)
1862 BC	Jacob (son of Isaac, brother to Esau, name changed to Israel)
1771 BC	Joseph (first son of Jacob and Rachel, sold into Egypt)
1597 BC	Moses (descendant of Israel, born 135 years after Israelites came to Egypt, raised as Egyptian Prince, freed the Israelites from bondage)
1470 BC	Joshua (descendant of Israel, helped lead Israelites into the Promised Land)
1079 BC	Samuel (prophet of Israel)
1037 BC	Saul (king of Israel)
1032 BC	David (defeated Goliath; king of Israel)
962 BC	Solomon (son of David; king of Israel)

YEAR	EVENT
922 BC	The kingdom of Israel is divided into the Northern Kingdom (Israel) and the Southern Kingdom (Judah)
	Elijah the prophet
	Jonah
722 BC	The Northern Kingdom of Israel is captured and taken captive by the Assyrians. They never return as a group
587 BC	The Southern Kingdom of Judah is taken captive to Babylon. The temple is destroyed
	Daniel and the lion's den
538 BC	Jewish captives are allowed to return to Jerusalem and rebuild their temple
	Esther, queen of Persia

Map of Ancient Israel

MAJOR CITIES AND AREAS STUDIED IN LESSONS

Sources

Benson, Ezra T. "The Great Commandment—Love the Lord." *Ensign*, May 1988.

Church Educational System. *Old Testament Student Manual.* (Salt Lake City: The Church of Jesus Christ of Latter-day Saints, 1981.)

Faust, James E. "Where Do I Make My Stand?" *Ensign*, November 2004.

Hafen, Bruce C. Hafen and Marie K. "Crossing Thresholds and Becoming Equal Partners." *Ensign*, Aug. 2007.

Jackson, Kent P. *Joseph Smith's commentary on the Bible.* (Salt Lake: Deseret Book, 1994.)

Ludlow, Daniel H. *A Companion to Your Study of the Old Testament.* (Salt Lake City: Deseret Book, 1981.)

McConkie, Bruce R. *Mormon Doctrine.* Salt Lake: Deseret Book, 1989.

Ridges, David J. *The Old Testament Made Easier Vol. 1–3.* (Springville, Utah: Cedar Fort, Inc., 2005.)

Seely, David Rolph. "I Have a Question." *Ensign*, Jan. 1994, 54.

Skousen, W. Cleon. *The First Two Thousand Years.* (Salt Lake City: Bookcraft, 1953.)

—. *The Fourth Thousand Years.* (Salt Lake: Bookcraft, 1966.)

—. *The Third Thousand Years.* (Salt Lake City: Bookcraft, 1964.)

Smoot, Mary Ellen. "For Such a Time As This." *Ensign*, Oct. 1997.

Taylor, John. Old Testament Student Manual, 1980: 56.

About the Author

Janet Burningham was born and raised in Provo, Utah. After graduating from Brigham Young University with a bachelor's degree in elementary education, she taught school for several years and also developed curriculum for various educational programs. Currently she teaches special education at an elementary school.

Janet and her husband, Scott, are the parents of four children: Joshua, Katey, Madeline, and Benjamin.

She enjoys teaching and researching gospel topics, along with reading, walking, enjoying the outdoors, and spending time with family and friends.

You can visit her blog, Monday Nights, at jburningham.blogspot.com.

0 26575 53771 0